# MYANMAR

## Democratisation, Foreign Policy and Elections

# MYANMAR

## Democratisation, Foreign Policy and Elections

*Edited by*

Amrita Dey

*Foreword by*

Subir Bhaumik

Former BBC Bureau Chief (East & Northeast India)

MAULANA ABUL KALAM AZAD INSTITUTE OF ASIAN STUDIES
KOLKATA

PENTAGON PRESS

**Myanmar: Democratisation, Foreign Policy and Elections**
*Editor: Amrita Dey*

ISBN 978-81-8274-879-8

First Published in 2016



*Published by*
PENTAGON PRESS
206, Peacock Lane, Shahpur Jat,
New Delhi-110049
Phones: 011-64706243, 26491568
Telefax: 011-26490600
email: rajan@pentagonpress.in
website: www.pentagonpress.in

Branch
Flat No.213, Athena-2,
Clover Acropolis,
Viman Nagar,
Pune-411014
Email: pentagonpresspune@gmail.com

Printed at Aegean Offset Printers, Greater Noida, U.P.

# Contents

# Contributors

1. **Dr. Amrita Dey,** Fellow, MAKAIAS.
2. **Prof. Eshanul Haque,** Professor, Department of International Relations, University of Dhaka, Bangladesh.
3. **Dr. Jabin T. Jacob,** Assistant Director and Fellow, Institute of Chinese Studies, New Delhi.
4. **Yukteshwar Kumar,** Chinese Course Director, Bath University, London.
5. **Sayantani Sen Majumdar,** Fellow, MAKAIAS.
6. **U Hla Myint,** Former Ambassador to Australia, Myanmar Institute of Strategic and International Studies, Yangon.
7. **Laldinkima Sailo,** Research Associate, Institute of South Asian Studies (ISAS), Singapore.
8. **Pongkwan Sawasdipakdi,** Lecturer, Faculty of Political Science, Thammasat University, Thailand.
9. **Amb. V. Sundararajan Seshadri,** Vice-Chairman, RIS and former Ambassador of India to Myanmar.
10. **U Myo Yan Naing Thein,** Director, BAYDA Institute and Deputy Head (Central Research Department, National League for Democracy), Myanmar.
11. **U Khin Maung Win,** Former Deputy Foreign Minister, MISIS, Yangon.
12. **Dr. K.Yhome,** Fellow, Observer Research Foundation, New Delhi.

# Foreword

The seminar on Myanmar's future, held a few months before the historic Nov 10 2015 Parliament elections, provided a unique platform to discuss which way the Pagoda Nation was headed and what would that mean for India. It brought together a unique mix of scholars and practitioners from both India and Myanmar and at least two who hailed from India's Northeast, which has a direct stake in the way Myanmar shapes up in the years ahead. This volume that emerges from the discussions in that seminar (*Myanmar: Moving Towards Elections on 19-20 February, 2015*) is timely. On 10 November 2015, Myanmar had its first free and fair polls since 1990. The results were similar – a sweep by Aung Sang Suu Kyi's National League for Democracy in 2015, 25 years after the 1990 polls, has proved that Myanmar's urge for democracy has far outweighed other concerns raised during the polls. The military junta's remote control and the focus on religious fundamentalism raised by its political cronies failed to stop the NLD in its victory march.

But unlike 1990, the military junta has refrained from brinksmanship, perhaps because it is in no position to ignore the sweeping mandate of the Myanmar people. The fact that the Myanmar electorate have decisively voted for the NLD in 1990 and 2015 has gone a long way to strengthen the cause of democracy in Myanmar. While in 1990, the junta refused to acknowledge the poll verdict and refused to hand over the reins of the government to Suu Kyi, it has acknowledged the poll verdict in 2015. Former junta chief Than Shwe, who is still believed to remote-control the military establishment, has even gone as far as saying that "Suu Kyi will lead the nation without any doubt".

But much as I had stressed during my presentation at the MAKAIS seminar, I would reiterate here that the Myanmar military establishment is a political animal with a strong strategic instinct of how to hang on to power. The 2008 constitution it worked out gives it control of three crucial ministries (Interior, Defence and Border Affairs) and 25 percent of the seats in the Partliament. The constitution also ensures Suu Kyi will not be President unless the Art 59(f) is amended. So when Than Shwe said Suu Kyi *will* (emphasis) lead the nation, he seemed to be pointing to the future, not the present. That gives the Tatmadaw ( the Burmese military) some breathing space, some time to strategise how to deny the inevitable and seek an honorable exit .

Aung Sang Suu Kyi's angst burst in the open after the polls when she made it clear that she and not the President would run the country. Suu Kyi knows the world recognizes her mandate – and cannot overlook her undiminished public appeal 25 years after she first swept the Parliament polls in Myanmar. But as she heads into one round of dialogue after another to ensure transfer of power, she will run into a group of seasoned political warriors, in and out of uniform, who are at their best when in strategic retreat. Suu Kyi is aware of the challenge – which is why she told India Today TV in a frank interview that she was a 'practical politician' and not an 'icon'. To which she did not fail to add: "Icons sit on walls and do nothing."

The years ahead are crucial for Myanmar. Whether democracy returns to the much tortured land depends on how the NLD negotiates the transfer of power in the months ahead. But whether it is institutionalized would depend on constitutional amendments that were suggested during the Thein Sein regime and rejected in Parliament. There can be no authentic democracy in Myanmar if the army retains 25 percent of the seats in Parliament – or three crucial ministries – and if Art 59(f) is not dropped.

But Myanmar's future as a nation-state also depends on how it addresses the federal question. Thein Sein's government failed to get most of the ethnic rebel groups in the nationwide ceasefire agreement. Much would depend on whether a NLD government manages to get all ethnic rebel militias into a ceasefire and then resolve the federal issue through a fresh Panglong type process or otherwise. One should never forget that if the rebellions erupt again, the Tatmadaw gets a chance for a de facto control of the reins of power through some kind of a national emergency mechanism.

So the challenge for Suu Kyi is to address the questions of democracy and federalism as one holistic question. That will not be easy. Much also depends on the role played by the West, China, India and the Association of Southeast Asian Nations (ASEAN). If the West quietly boost the Myanmar military to counter China as they have backed the Pakistan military for a whole host of strategic reasons, Suu Kyi may find her democracy agenda betrayed by the very countries she might count on. India's role will thus become crucial and if she wants to be counted as a power to reckon with in South-east Asia in future, she will have to play a crucial role in restoration of democracy and federalism in Myanmar. After all, India's own tryst with destiny and relative success in preserving democracy and federalism will make her, rather than the West, a more effective model for Myanmar to emulate. But her current level of presence in Myanmar is poor and that needs to change, not the least because Myanmar is our land bridge to South-east Asia and crucial to the success of our 'Act East' policy.

The articles in this MAKAIS volume will surely help readers understand some of these challenges to Myanmar's future.

SUBIR BHAUMIK

# Introduction

On 28 November 2007 the Association of Southeast Asian Nations (ASEAN) signed the Charter that confirmed ASEAN's status as an intergovernmental organization with legal personality and its commitment to a range of ambitious goals. Among the many clauses are the ones relating to strengthening democracy, enhancing good governance and the rule of law, promoting and protecting human rights and fundamental freedoms.

These developments within the Association are particularly important at a time when Thailand's military that seized power in May 2014 are unwilling to relinquish it, and the society there has begun to look more chaotic, messy (economically) and frustration among the Thai nationals are high. Like Thailand, Malaysia's slide from an authoritarian to a totalitarian UNMO rule cannot be halted. "Today's Malaysia," says an expert "is a more dangerous place, quite like Pakistan and Yemen through the infusion of horribly arcane and extremist Islamic ideology." Likewise, Indonesia's deregulation packages (with little interest in diplomacy and regional politics) under the leadership of President Jokowi Widodo's remains highly elusive. Among the other members of the Association, Brunei Darussalam is an absolute sultanate and in the states of Laos and Vietnam, the Communist parties still hold its sway. Democracy in the Philippines is constrained by serious impediments to inclusiveness and participation, rampant corruption and absence of the rule of law, with continuing influence of the military and business elites in shaping government policies.

It's for ASEAN'S sake that Myanmar needs to be on track—on its road to genuine democratic transition. The Association, although, it never used 'democracy' as a condition for its membership; but it is quietly practicing it as a 'prerequisite' to remain within the family. The ASEAN Charter, for instance, lists as one of the purposes of ASEAN 'To ensure that the members of the Association live in peace with the world at large in a just, democratic and harmonious environment; to adhere to the rule of law, principles of democracy and good governance; requiring all member states under it to take necessary measures to implement its provisions, failing which, would constitute a breach of the Charter.*

Myanmar too needs ASEAN to regionally prove its commitment to continuing democratic reforms, justice and equality; to address the economic difficulties faced by the people of the country. As also to use its membership within the Association to remain a part of the ASEAN family (promoting its integration efforts and the establishment of the ASEAN Community) than be a buffer state sandwiched between two great powers." The great powers here being China and Washington, with Beijing being increasingly wary of Washington's motive to contain China's rise as a regional military and economic power: while Washington is increasingly getting vocal about China's assertive behavior towards the regional neighbors, as also its use of supposed network of commercial and military access points in the Indian Ocean Region to counterbalance USA's 'pivot' to Asia.

Myanmar, at this juncture, would find it congenial to 'play it safe' (as its past experiences show) to promote its three strategic goals, including external security, to work towards a stable and peaceful country, and build a modern and developed state that will be respected internationally.** Prime Minister U NU, on the eve of Burma's independence, once rightly said: "On behalf of my country, I extend my tender greetings to other nations, with all of whom we hope to live forever on terms of amity and concord. Burma greets them all; wishes well of them, and offer her cooperation in the tasks of making a greater and nobler world and in securing and preserving the cause of perpetual peace for this harassed world."

The two days International Conference at Maulana Abul Kalam Azad Institute of Asian Studies, Kolkata, India, discussed and debated issues relating to democratization and Myanmar's preparedness for the 2015 election. It also dealt with Myanmar's bilateral relationship with China, Thailand, Bangladesh and India, though of consequence politically (only),

---

*For better understanding see Melissa Crouch and Tim Lindsey (ed.) Law, Society and Transition in Myanmar, Hart Publishing, 2014.

**For better understanding see Jurgen Haacke: Myanmar and the United States: Prospects for a Limited Security Partnership, The United States Studies Centre, November 2015.

in an attempt to place Myanmar's foreign policy objectives within the broader regional and global context. This being extremely important at a time when Myanmar has adopted a 'diversification strategy' in its foreign policy to break-free from the Chinese 'clutch' in order to recast its relationship with regional/extra-regional partners, including Japan, India, Russia, USA and Europe; using them in turn, to become, important stakeholders in Myanmar's reform process across a range of areas, including capacity building, good governance and the peace process.

The first three papers examines the domestic issues in Myanmar with a particular focus on challenges inherited by the country from history and those that grew out of the reforms undertaken by the present government in power since 2011. **Myo Yan Naung Thein's** paper on *Myanmar: Dictatorship to Democracy and Development* examines Burma's transition from dictatorship to democracy, ending decades of isolation and now actively re-engaging with the global economy. But, Burma according to Myo Yan is still not very changed. Civil war and ethno-religious conflicts are threatening the stability of the country. Infrastructures are many decades old; corruption is still rampant and rule of law is still absent. Inflation, unemployment, shortage of electricity and confiscated land problems are major challenges. Important ministerial posts are still automatically filled-in by senior military officers and there is a serious debate in Burma over the nature of federalism. Given that transitions are never smooth, Myo Thein feels that the need of the hour is to engage' with Burma from outside: while internally, it needs to push for structural changes from the bottom up, as political leadership works to push reforms from the top down. He proposed three strategies: Human Rights Protection and Promotion Strategy, Poverty Alleviation Strategy and Sustainable Development Strategy: these strategies being used as guides to translate the agendas into implementable policies, programs and projects at all levels of society. **Khin Maung Win's** paper on *Myanmar's Political Landscape: A Profile* discusses the reform process in Myanmar under the leadership of President Thein Sein since he assumed power in 2011. Although there was an initial skepticism, says U Win, Myanmar has undergone positive changes during this period, despite having many complex issues and challenges. Outstanding among them being the armed struggle among its ethnic communities; the issue of changing particular Articles in the 2008 Constitution, the establishment of a federal system, the implementation of various reform processes including education reforms, among others. The paper ends by looking at 2015 as a critical year in Myanmar's history as the results of the general election holds the key to strengthen the democratic system and institutions in the nation. **U Hla Myint**'s paper on

*General Elections, Peace Process of Myanmar and Their Implications* critically examines two subjects—the 2015 general elections and the peace process of Myanmar, as speculations abound these two events. The failure to do free and fair elections as scheduled, according to U Myint, and lack of progress in signing the nationwide ceasefire with armed ethnic organizations may undermine the confidence of the International community, as well as jeopardize the political stability and smooth transition of the country. It is also the most important event for the Myanmarese people due to its impact on the future of the country as well as on their lives; while the peace process is designed to settle questions of nationality once and for all, necessitating firm commitment of all the stakeholders in reaching its desired outcome.

The second set of three papers examines Myanmar's bilateral relationship with India. **Laldinkima Sailo's** paper on *Perception on India-Myanmar Relations* identifies elite perceptions and public opinion as the two main factors that exert a growing influence on the policymakers who engage in taking bilateral relations forward. In Myanmar, according to Mr. Sailo, with the growth of infrastructure and natural resources, involvement of civil society, community groups and free media—public opinion has become stronger to reckon with. But when it comes to India and Myanmar relations, the two countries continue to be mired by several (mis)-perceptions, including (1) Feeling of neglect and hostility on part of India for Myanmar. The omission of invitation to President Thein Sein in the swearing ceremony of Indian Prime Minister Narendra Modi; (2) India as a democracy is considered as 'slow' due to its tardy implementation policies; (3) Inevitable comparison with China, which is seen as dynamic and competitive; (4) Forays by Indian companies provide a sense of lack of understanding of Myanmar's market. While Chinese goods and brands dot the markets of Myanmar, India is not seen in the nearest proximity; (5) Border Trade with India account even less than Bangladesh and border 'dispute' depreciate much of the neighborhood relations; (6) Lack of initiative from both sides to implement and resolve multi-modal projects like the Kaladan Project and other connectivity issues. **K.Yhome's** paper on *Re-Imaging Neighborhood Ties: Looking Beyond Bilateralism* analyses the geographical proximity between Bangladesh, India and Myanmar that lays a strong basis for trilateralism among the three countries: as internal and external factors are opening up huge opportunities for them to work together in the interest of each other and the wider Bay of Bengal region. Trilateralism that can be practiced through the promotion of "growth triangles" and in the maritime security arena, through exchange in capacity building and information sharing regarding threats of piracy, terrorism, gunrunning and trafficking in the region. **Sayantani Sen Majumdar's** paper on *North-East Region: Connecting India and Myanmar* examines Phase 2 of India's Look East Policy (LEP) as it emphasizes the development of its North-East Region (NER) because of its geographic, demographic, political, economic, cultural and religious proximity to South East Asia (SEA). As NER bears direct surface connection with SEA either through Bangladesh or Myanmar, the relevance of its geography in promoting India-Myanmar bonhomie multiplies, despite fears of an aggressive China; in getting Myanmar government to come down heavily on the North-Eastern insurgents and rebel groups taking refuge inside their borders; for better trade and transit facilities, including the exploration of Myanmar's vibrant gas, oil and energy resources.

The third set of four papers looks into Myanmar's bilateral relationship with China, Thailand and Bangladesh. **Jabin Jacob's** paper on *China and Myanmar Elections: plus ca change, plus cest la meme chose*? analyses Myanmar's tryst with democracy and its preparedness for the 2015 elections. And the impact it will have on China. From China's perspective, says the author, there are certainly issues that hold consequences for not just China's external relations but also for its domestic affairs. China has been thinking of 'managing' or dealing with the consequences or spillover of the political changes in Myanmar. But no matter what the results of Myanmar's elections, China has its broad strategy chalked out to ensure that Myanmar remains a stable, peaceful country that provides opportunities for its interests to flourish both through 'traditional' and 'non-traditional' initiatives. **Pongkwan Sawasdipakdi's** paper on *Thailand's Policy Towards Myanmar: A Way to Gain International Legitimacy* combines two approaches in analyzing Thailand's foreign policy towards Myanmar, one imposed by international-level elements during the Cold War. As a result, the Thai ruling elites decided to bandwagon with the United States. However towards the end of the Cold War external pressure on Thailand's foreign policy towards Myanmar gradually declined and became limited: the second imposed by domestic factors owing to a combination of structural reasons and role of the Thai elites. However since 2010, the trend of Thailand's foreign policy towards Myanmar has taken a positive trajectory, given the multidimensional economic interests that prevent complete interruption of bilateral relationship between these two neighbors. **Ehsanul Haque's** paper on *Bangladesh's Relations with a Changing Myanmar: Determinants, Dynamics, Constraints and Promises* argues that as Myanmar opens up and prepares for election, Bangladesh finds the country to be extremely critical in revamping its bilateral trade and economic cooperation, fostering connectivity, and enhancing people-to-people contact/Track II diplomacy, perhaps more so now than ever before. From Bangladesh's perspective, Myanmar's evolving dynamics, coupled with its growing regional role and international stand, calls for a new Bangladesh-Myanmar understanding and partnership – one that breaks out of past difficulties and promises to move forward: sans limitations and challenges in their bilateral relations, including the Rohingya question, border tension and skirmishes, cross-border crime and terrorism. The author strongly feels that the advent of a new civilian government in Myanmar and developments in Bangladesh presents a window of opportunity for both the countries to pragmatically pursue their mutually beneficial relationship. **Yukteshwar Kumar's** paper on *The India Factor in Sino-Myanmar Relations* seeks to answer and examine China's existing strategic relation with Myanmar and what role India shall play in the changing atmosphere after the general elections in Naypyidaw. In the last two decades, India lost the opportunity to cement its ties with Myanmar, while China edged it out during this period through its soft power, trade and economic ties in the region. But India, according to the author, has more advantage over China, including their closer cultural, religious and historical affinities. Indian democracy is also admired by majority of Myanmar people while the Chinese are despised by many as the 'exploiter of their economy' and for making selfish benefit. The volume concludes with **Amrita Dey's** observation on Myanmar's overall preparedness for the 2015 elections and the way it wants to work towards a 'disciplined flourishing democracy' making it a top-down approach with wider space for rule of law and civil liberty. It also examines the role of regional and extra-regional countries with a hope that anything less than a viable transition in Myanmar would seriously upset the Buddhist doctrine of *Kalama Sutta* and a vibrant scholarly community that has found a reason to explore and study this country often tagged as 'blessed with and bedeviled by diversity'.

**Amrita Dey**

# Keynote Address
# India-Myanmar Relations: As Myanmar Embarks on Reform and Development

*V.S. Seshadri*[1]

Chairman of MAKAIAS, Shri Sitaram Sharma,
Consul-General of Myanmar, U Than Htwe,
Amb. Krishnan Srinivasan, former Foreign Secretary,
Former Deputy Foreign Minister of Myanmar, **U Khin Maung Win**,
Director of MAKAIAS, Dr Sreeradha Dutta,
Distinguished Delegates, Ladies and Gentlemen.

It is a privilege and a honour for me to speak to such a distinguished group of researchers and analysts on Myanmar. Having served there for almost three years, it has become, for me, an exciting country of interest. My term there beginning from July 2010, more or less coincided with the beginning of the active phase of the transition process towards a Constitutional Republic. I could have a ringside view of the many developments then and I am happy to share my perspectives. 2015, and the elections scheduled for later this year, have the potential to provide further consolidation to what appears to be an irreversible process towards further exploration and search for Myanmar's own version of democracy. The Maulana Abul Kalam Azad Institute of Asian Studies (MAKAIAS), Kolkata has always taken an active interest in studying Myanmar. It could not have chosen a more opportune time to analyse and examine this topic. I thank the institute, the Chairman, Shri Sitaram Sharma, Director Professor Sreeradha Dutta and Dr Amrita Dey for inviting me to share my thoughts on this occasion. It would also be most interesting to hear the views of several distinguished scholars including those from Myanmar participating in this conference.

During my talk, I shall broadly focus on two aspects. One will relate to the transition process under way in Myanmar and what possibly constitutes the dynamics and the various elements that may determine its further outcome. Secondly, I would also like to dwell on the bilateral relations between our two neighbouring countries and focus on what could be certain aspects that could help to further strengthen what is already a multi-faceted relationship.

Taking up the transition first, as I landed in Myanmar on July 2010, I could see the events unfolding systematically. First was the registration of political parties according to a timetable and announcement of the election schedule in August with the elections to take place in November that year. All senior functionaries of the government who were military officers relinquished their uniforms and became civilians but for Senior General Than Shwe and Vice-Senior General Maung Aye. The elections themselves were held when the diplomats including myself were taken around as observers. The general feeling was, there was a plan, there was a method to it as it happened, such as when the new flag prescribed in the Constitution went up one day without any prior announcement. And the people absorbed them all as they came, even as they may or may not have endorsed them. Holding elections was Step 5 of the Seven Step Road map[2] adopted by the military regime, for transition towards a 'discipline flourishing democracy'; The first four steps included drawing up of the Constitution and holding a referendum all of which had already been completed by 2008. The outcome of these elections which resulted in 78 per cent of the contested seats being won by the military-backed Union Solidarity and Development Party (USDP) was not a surprise, considering the circumstances at that time when the real opposition was not part of the contest. But the huge turnout was reflecting the people's eagerness to participate in any such opening up despite there being some calls for staying away from the polls.

Immediately after the elections, Daw Aung San Suu Kyi was released from house arrest (the sentence period also came to an end) giving rise to the possibility that this time the changes could be somewhat more real. Her presence lent an altogether new dimension to the political scenario, with her beginning to participate in the activities of her party, the National League for Democracy (NLD), and in meeting the diplomats and visiting leaders from abroad.

Meanwhile, the two houses of Parliament convened—the Sixth Step of the Road Map—and the Lower and Upper House Speakers were elected. There was certainly some surprise at the naming of the Lower House Speaker Thura U Shwe Mann who had been rumoured as having been identified for the highest post. The two Houses of Parliament went through the process of electing the various Parliamentary Committees and the three Vice-Presidents. One of them, the former Prime Minister Thein Sein, was also elected the President. During this period, while the two Houses of Parliament gave their formal approval to many nominations, there was little debate or discussion. On occasions, the Parliament session would convene at 10.00 am and adjourn by 10.30 am, once it had approved some nominations. The Press was not allowed free access, and only the official media showed some photo shots in news bulletins. In brief, therefore, while there was change, it all appeared going according to a plan with no scope for any among the opposition to have a substantive say, and with no clue given about the choice of one nominee over another.

Then came the time for the launch of the Seventh Step of the Road Map which said, 'The leaders, government and authoritative bodies elected to Parliament shall continue with the task of constructing a new state'. There were then doubts if Senior General Than Shwe and Vice-Senior General Maung Aye would continue to hold on to their military posts but these doubts too were soon cleared with the nomination of a new Commander-in-Chief of Armed Forces and the two military leaders making a total exit from public view. And to this day, this continues to be the case.

## The President's Path-Breaking Inaugural Speeches

And then on 30th March 2011, the newly elected President Thein Sein and members of his cabinet were sworn into office. In what were path-breaking speeches addressed to the combined houses of Parliament (Pyidaungsu Hluttaw) on 30th March 2011, and to all the ministers, deputy ministers and other Union level Organisations on 31st March 2011, he laid out the tasks and responsibilities that would be carried forward by his government. The President said that the most important task of his administration was to create good governance and clean government. The second task was to bring the democratic practices that make the legislature, executive and judicial pillars that emerge from the Constitution, to come to life. A third task was bringing in the rule of law to ensure speediness and effectiveness of government transactions. He said that they also had to respect the role of the media. He underlined that the government and its officials must abstain from corruption and bribery. All this was suddenly fresh air blowing, and the pronouncements suddenly brought greater hope and optimism. But there was scepticism as well, because most of the new ministers were there earlier too under the military regime, and only a few ministries like health and education were given to specialists with non-military background. Many wondered whether they will see a faithful implementation of the Presidential pronouncements.

Reviewing the developments now after almost four years since the non-military government took over, one can say that reforms have been initiated in several areas—political and ethnic affairs, internal peace and reconciliation and in the opening up of the economy. More importantly, people's views and protests have also come to influence decisions, like the suspension of work on the Myitsone Dam, the dialogue with Daw Aung San Suu Kyi that in turn influenced the release of political prisoners and changes in the electoral laws that would allow the National League for Democracy (NLD) to participate in the by-elections and win overwhelmingly, an enquiry launched about the Letpadaung Copper mine project following protests that in turn led to a reworking of the deal and so on. This was indeed a remarkable change as the personalities involved in the decision-making were not very different from the ones earlier.

Likewise, the Parliament has also come a long way from looking like a rubber stamp in the first session, to the ongoing eleventh session which is discussing constitutional reforms. And the debates are appearing reasonably open, questions are allowed to be asked on various topics and the media coverage, widening. To his credit, the Lower House Speaker Thura U Shwe Mann has taken a lead in guiding the change.

On the media front again, there is far greater openness. Privately owned newspapers and magazines that also carry views critical of the government are freely available. Of course, there are red lines and a draft media law is still doing the rounds for arriving at a consensus. Discussions about media freedom are also being accompanied by calls made by the government Spokesmen for media responsibility.

Most political prisoners have been released. Several leading exiles have also returned. With Daw Aung San Suu Kyi and the NLD joining the political process and the various debates, and making other contributions including in the form of the NLD leader chairing the Parliamentary Committee for Rule of Law, Peace and Tranquility, and in recent months the Lady raising her voice about the need for constitutional reform, have provided more substance to the discussions towards further democratic reform. Significant contributions are also being made by 1988 student activists, who have turned to become social activists willing to lend their voice and services for nation building. Several civil society organisations have also joined the fray and are making their contributions.

The ethnic reconciliation process is work in progress. Ceasefire agreements with most major groups have been arrived at, at the state level. But the six formal rounds of negotiations and many informal ones that have taken place between the Govt. Union Peace Making Working Committee and the National Central Coordinating Team of the armed ethnic groups for signing a nationwide ceasefire agreement have yet to bear fruit. While many issues have reportedly been resolved including a pledge to adopt a federal system, some differences still persist. These include seven or eight critical issues including those relating to the code of conduct, arrangements for monitoring ceasefire zones and the idea of a federal army . On the one hand, what is very positive is that one can now see leaders from the Karen National Union or other armed group outfits frequently visiting Nay Pyi Daw and talking to leaders from the government and the armed forces. But there are also concerns being expressed by a few others who have already reached agreements, but who feel that the time is being lost and the process is not moving forward further with some even alleging that government troops are not fully honouring their ceasefire commitments. Violent clashes meanwhile continue to be reported from the Kachin state and certain areas of the Shan State with renewed fighting in the Kokang area being the latest.

The so called 'Rohingya' related problem in the Rakhine State, and the communal clashes that have taken place there and in other parts of the country are issues that will need to be earnestly addressed both in the short term and in the long term. It would be important that these issues also do not get exacerbated during an election year.

On the economic reform front, there have been many welcome changes—the unification of exchange rates and the managed float of the *Kyat* with the International Monetary Fund collaboration, the clearing of Myanmar's external debt with the help of Japan and a few other donor countries that has enabled Myanmar to now receive ADB/World Bank assistance, the liberalisation of the banking sector that has seen many new domestic private banks and also a limited opening to foreign banks, the revision of the foreign trade policy, reforms in taxation, the launch of a new Foreign Investment Law, etc.; Telecom, Power, Airports expansion, exploration of onshore/offshore gas and petroleum blocks have also seen initiatives being taken. SEZs are also being sought to be developed in Thilawa, Dawei and Kyaukphyu in collaboration with foreign partners. The economic outlook projected by international agencies like the IMF or ADB appear quite positive. With Myanmar now registering an 8.25 percent growth, and expected to do similarly well in the coming years, the prospect of Myanmar becoming a middle income economy by the next decade appear very bright.

In international affairs, Myanmar's leaders have reached out to all countries to make friends, irrespective of their positions about Myanmar earlier. The international community has also responded well with many more countries now having embassies in Myanmar and by developing closer ties and removing or suspending most of the sanctions. Many countries have also come forward, offering technical and financial assistance. The growing economic opportunities are also a draw. The earlier preponderance of China in Myanmar's external relations has certainly diminished to some extent with the entry of other players even as China continues to play a very significant part. With Myanmar having hosted the South East Asian games in December 2013 and after having chaired the ASEAN in 2014 successfully, one can say that it is steadily moving towards being a part of the international mainstream.

Coming then to the theme of the Conference, which is 2015 and the elections in Myanmar, the year certainly promises to be interesting. The focus is now on three interrelated issues. First is the constitutional reforms, which is faced with some sensitive clauses including:

(a) Amendment of Article 59(f) which currently bars a Myanmarese national having children or other close relatives of different nationality to be elected as a President or Vice-President (Amending this article is critical to Daw Aung San Suu Kyi being able to bid for the top post);
(b) The 25 percent of reservation of the seats for the military in the Union and provincial legislatures and the three important ministries reserved for military nominees;
(c) Decentralisation and further sharing of powers between Central and State governments;
(d) Greater rights for ethnic minority areas and how the ethnic militia will be dealt with;
(e) A reduction in the high 75 per cent majority required for any constitutional amendment.

Another set of issues to be resolved are the electoral rules. While the Lower House of Parliament has already decided that it would stay with the present first-past-the-post system, the Upper House is still consulting with the Constitutional Tribunal about moving to a proportional representation system. Such a change in the system is being opposed by many of the ethnic parties as also by the NLD. There is also an intense debate currently underway about eligibility of the 'white card' holders to vote. While they all voted in the 2010 elections and in the 2008 referendum, this has become a new issue that has come to the fore particularly because of the so-called Rohingya problem.

A third set of issues that is also related with the elections, concerns the resolution of the ethnic issue and whether a ceasefire agreement can still be reached and a political dialogue launched before this year-end. Elections could not be held in some of these areas in 2010 because of continuing disturbances.

As it appears, there are four Presidential hopefuls viz., the incumbent President Thein Sein, who has not ruled himself out of the race, the Lower House Speaker Thura Shwe Mann, the NLD Leader Daw Aung San Suu Kyi who, of course, will be eligible only if Article 59(f) is amended and the Commander-in-Chief of the Armed Forces Senior General Min Aung Hlaing, who is expected to retire next year. Recently, when he was asked if he will join politics, the Armed Forces Chief responded that he will decide depending on the situation at the time.

These key players have been taking different positions on the key questions of constitutional reform on which a referendum, it now appears, will be held in May this year. But it is still unclear what are the issues that will be put up for approval in the referendum. Daw Aung San Suu Kyi has been most vocal in calling for constitutional reform and her party is keen on doing away with the role of the military in governance, and in modifying both Article 59(f) and Article 436 on the requirement of a three-fourth majority.

At the other extreme has been the armed forces chief who has been quoted as saying that Myanmar is not yet ready for a reduced military role in the Parliament and the country is still a young democracy. He has further stated that the reform process should not be hasty, but rather a step-by-step process in which the military will collaborate to amend the Constitution if the people wanted to amend it.

The President himself has been more keen on prioritising the ethnic peace process and has said that the national ceasefire agreement has been vital to moving forward towards political dialogue which aims to build the union based on flourishing democracy and federalism. The President has also echoed the views of the Armed forces chief about the military's role saying that Myanmar at this stage was a 'nascent' democracy and that Myanmar's army will step back from its prominent role in the government once peace agreements are reached with insurgent groups. On constitutional reform, again, he has pointed out that any reform must be carried out step by step by the Parliament and approved by a national referendum.

The Speaker himself has not given his individual views on the various reforms but has been a key proponent of holding a national referendum in May for which the Parliament will soon have to decide on the amendments that need to be put up in place. He has also been supportive of a limited six-party dialogue; comprising the President, the Armed Forces Chief, the two speakers, Daw Aung San Suu Kyi and a representative of the ethnic groups to confer and come to an understanding on reforms before they are taken up by the Parliament. Daw Aung San Suu Kyi was in fact the first to call for such a limited dialogue although she had proposed a four-party dialogue that had involved only the President, the Armed Forces Chief, the Lower House Speaker and herself. But the six-party dialogue has now been endorsed by the Lower House and she seems to be agreeable to it. It is however not clear if such a limited dialogue meeting will indeed be held.

Piecing all these various views and developments together, one can perhaps summarise the overall scene thus:

(i) Firstly, all the parties seem agreed on the need for reform of the Constitution, and an eventual reduction of role of the military, although the pace and *inter se* prioritisation are seeing significant differences in approach;

(ii) Constitutional reforms providing greater ethnic rights, providing a formulation for a federal union that seems now to be agreed in principle, etc., may all have to wait till a national ceasefire agreement is signed and the political dialogue that is to follow is able to arrive at an understanding;

(iii) Till the ethnic peace issue is settled, it seems unlikely that the military will agree to any reduction in its role. Scholars here may perhaps be interested in a recent paper by Robert H. Taylor, published by the Institute for South East Asia Studies in Singapore, in which he argues that the formation of an acceptable government after the 2015 elections, and the ongoing efforts to reach a political settlement with the country's numerous armed ethnic groups will determine the speed and the degree to which the armed forces will be willing to allow their autonomous role to be undermined or terminated; and

(iv) The Constitution reforms that may be approved for the May referendum may therefore be quite limited in scope and whether they will include an amendment to Article 59(f) is unclear.

While you can take an overall view on the movement in Myanmar towards democracy depending on whether you see the glass as half-full or half-empty, two aspects are encouraging. One is how far the transition has come in these four years—after 50 years of military rule, particularly compared to the scenario that I prescribed at the beginning of my talk. And the second, is an increasing evidence that views of the people are getting factored into decision-making as in the resolution of the recent education law issue, which saw country wide demonstration by students, but on which after four months of stand-off there is now an agreement to move ahead in reforming the law that had been passed by the Parliament in September or on the white card issue on which again the government is seen as giving into popular opinion. Of course, critics have referred to certain aspects like the continued top–down approach to decision-making—there being very little decentralisation of decision-making to region and state levels—the need for judicial reform, the lack of a fair administration of the rule of law and continued favours being given to crony companies, etc.; these will certainly need attention in due course of time.

Let me now turn to the second focus of my talk which is to look at how our bilateral relations are progressing. I do not have to elaborate to this well-informed audience about our multifaceted ties that have deep historical and civilisational roots. Or indeed, about the long maritime and land borders that we share that have for long been used by monks and merchants and which continue to hold great promise for closer ties. While there are many aspects that one can dwell on, I shall try to be brief with three pointed remarks about recent trends.

First of note would be the strengthening of India's bilateral ties with Myanmar now moving towards a democratic framework. On the political front, it is a welcome sign that the exchange of high-level visits are now more frequent; the latest being the goodwill visit of Myanmarese Vice President Sai Mauk Kham to India last month. Prime Minister Narendra Modi visited Myanmar last November for the ASEAN-related meetings and an indication was given at that time that a bilateral visit by him may perhaps take place this year. It will be important to keep up this momentum.

The second aspect that I would like to point out is the generally increasing recognition of how the well-being and development of Northeast India and of western Myanmar can be mutually reinforcing. The Kaladan project, the highway connectivity between Imphal and Mandalay and the proposal for a bus service, a good road link between Mizoram and the Chin state and a better road and railway connectivity within Northeast India are all at different stages of implementation and have the potential to make a sea change towards facilitating mobility of goods, services and tourists. An early implementation of all these projects can bring enormous gains to people on both sides of the border. If they are also coupled with modernisation of the border trading framework, putting in place of the necessary soft infrastructure for smooth transit and transport and transformation of the emerging connectivity corridors into development corridors, then they can bring about win–win partnerships. Needless to add, however, that to make these happen, both sides will also have to tackle the unsettling security and insurgency situation with insurgents continuing to take shelter across the borders. A strengthened cooperation and building further on mutual confidence and trust can help realise the interrelated peace, connectivity and development dividends that remain to be harnessed. These objectives appear in harmony with Myanmar's autonomous moves towards greater openness, democratisation and economic reform as also the steps it is taking to achieve peace with the ethnic groups nationally.

A third aspect that I would like to highlight is the concern arising from a relatively lower profile of India in harnessing the growing trade and investment opportunities in Myanmar. India today ranks seventh among Myanmar's import sources and eleventh among foreign investors. Indian companies are yet to conclude major investment deals apart from the four Indian companies which have, among others, secured seven onshore/offshore hydrocarbon exploratory blocks for exploration. Indian companies, however, do not figure in any large infrastructure or manufacturing initiatives even as several other East Asian and South East Asian countries do. Three Indian banks have set up representative offices but no Indian commercial bank has figured among the nine licenses awarded last year to foreign banks to open local branches. Compare this with the fifties and early sixties when seven Indian commercial banks operated in Myanmar before they were all nationalised in 1963. India's Shipping Corporation of India has begun a welcome six-month trial run of a Colombo-Chennai (Krishnapatnam)-Yangon direct container service but there is a risk that if it fails to become economically viable soon, it may fold up. Air India, the only Indian airline with a direct connection, too is taking hesitant steps to increase its direct services from a tri-weekly Yangon-Kolkata-Bodhgaya service to an additional Delhi–Yangon weekly flight. This is even as Yangon is now connected by twelve flights every day from Bangkok, six every day from Singapore, five from Malaysia, four from China and one each daily from Tokyo, Seoul and Hanoi. Tourist arrivals in Myanmar exceeded 3 million in 2014.

Indian business chambers and other export promotion councils do mount delegations to Myanmar and also hold product displays from time to time. Some Indian business groups are also establishing local offices to scout for business. But this may be a time to move beyond incrementalism. It will be important to devise a strategy that also builds on India's development cooperation programmes. Efforts are needed to try and make the cost of doing business with Myanmar more competitive. Private initiatives will not succeed without some governmental backing and bank-financing support. Higher level visits will need to keep this perspective in mind.

Myanmar, I would stress here, is not just another business opportunity. It is also a strategically positioned neighbour. It would be important for India to go the extra mile in ensuring greater participation of Indian businesses in Myanmar's accelerated trade and investment initiatives. I would also consider that it would be in Myanmar's interest as well to enable greater Indian participation in its business activities. It is very welcome in this regard that our Minister of State for Commerce and Industry Shrimati Nirmala Sitharaman visited Myanmar earlier this week when many of trade and other related issues appear to have been discussed.

Distinguished delegates,

I am sure that the many speakers who will address this conference will share their perspectives on some of the aspects that I have referred to as also others that merit greater attention. I wish to congratulate the organisers of the conference for bringing together all the scholars and wish the deliberations everysucess.

## NOTES

1. Vice-Chairman, RIS and former Ambassador of India to Myanmar
2 The Seven Step Roadmap to Discipline Flourishing Democracy comprised
    1. to reassemble the National Convention;
    2. to implement requisite tasks for the founding of the democratic system;
    3. to draw up a constitution on principles advocated by the National Convention;
    4. to hold a national referendum;
    5. to hold free and fair elections;
    6. to convene the meeting of the elected representatives to the Hluttaw; and
    7. the leaders, government and authoritative bodies elected by the Hluttaw to continue with the task of constructing a new democratic state.

# 1

# Burma (Myanmar): Dictatorship to Democracy and Development

*Myo Yan Naung Thein*

*After decades of isolation, Burma is now actively re-engaging with the global economy. For successful re-engagement, Burma needs to implement comprehensive economic and political reforms. The still nascent transition in the country has emerged as one of the most promising efforts at democratisation in the world today. But, there are terrible violations of human rights in Burma and the question is how to prevent such repetitions in future. Among the most urgent priorities are resolving the ethnic and sectarian conflicts, creating jobs for the vast majority of the population, tackling corruption and establishing the rule of law. An important element of strong, democratic societies is adherence to the rule of law, which in turn depends on a strong constitution that has a broad public support. A political transition in itself is not enough to achieve ethnic equality; how to define federalism must be seriously debated in Burma. I am a Burmese political activist working for the democratisation of Burma for more than 20 years. Studying Burma has been my lifelong interest and, in this paper, I will be looking at what went wrong, what is happening currently and what should be done for the betterment of the country. I have analysed the economic and political conditions in Burma. In this paper, I propose three strategies: "Human Rights Protection and Promotion Strategy", "Poverty Alleviation Strategy" and "Sustainable Development Strategy". These strategies should be used as guidelines to translate these agendas into a set of implementable policies, programmes and projects. Civilians' participation would be the key to its success. Burma is facing challenges and needs the concerted effort of all its citizens. The relationship between democratisation, development and poverty reduction in Burma are interrelated and interdependent, and that requires mass involvement.*

## Burma

Burma is a beautiful country with 54.5 million people and is rich in natural resources. The country gained independence in 1948 which was followed by successive insurgencies and military coups. The military ruled Burma for nearly 50 years. Since 1962, once the Rice Bowl of Asia, Burma turned into one of the least developed countries. In 2010, President U Thein Sein's regime came into power and undertook unprecedented measures, including the release of political prisoners and giving some freedom to the people. After 2011, the National League for Democracy (NLD) contested the by-elections and Daw Aung San Suu Kyi entered the Parliament. The world leaders endorsed the reforms and started giving assistance to Burma and the country is now believed to be in transition from dictatorship to democracy and development.

But, Burma has not changed much. Civil war and ethnic and religious conflicts are threatening the stability of the country. The solutions to deforestation and environmental problems are pending. Corruption is still rampant and rule of law has not been restored as yet. Inflation, unemployment, shortage of electricity and confiscated land problems are major challenges. Important ministerial posts are still automatically filled by senior military officers. I am a Burmese political activist working for the democratisation of Burma for many years. I was imprisoned for nearly ten years and tortured until I became paralysed. Now I am working very closely with Daw Aung San Suu Kyi. Studying Burma has been my lifelong interest and I will be looking at what went wrong, what is happening and what should be done for the betterment of our country's future.

## Democracy

Democracy is more than just a set of specific government institutions; it rests upon a well-understood set of values, attitudes, and practices—all of which may take different forms and expressions among cultures and societies around the world. Democracies rest upon fundamental principles, not uniform practices. All democracies are systems in which the citizens are free to make political decisions and it is the rule of the majority. In a democratic society, majority rule must be coupled with guarantees of individual human rights that, in turn, serve to protect the rights of minorities and dissenters—whether ethnic or religious. The rights of minorities are protected because democratic laws and institutions protect the rights of all its citizens. Once this is accomplished, such groups can participate in, and contribute to, the country's democratic institutions. The principle of majority rule and minority rights are characteristics unique to all modern democracies, no matter how varied they are in terms of history, culture, population, and economy.[1]

## Poverty

According to the United Nations, poverty is denial of choices and opportunities, the violation of human dignity coupled with the lack of basic capacity to participate effectively in society; not having enough to eat and feed a family; not having a school or clinic to go to; not having any land on which to grow one's food or job to earn one's living and not having access to credit. It means insecurity, powerlessness and exclusion of individuals, households and communities. It means susceptibility to violence, and it often implies living in marginal or fragile environments, without access to clean water or sanitation. The social aspects of poverty may include lack of access to information, education, healthcare or political participation. According to the World Bank, reducing poverty is the fundamental objective of the economic development of the world.

## Development

The two most important ways of measuring development are economic development and human development. Economic development is the measure of a country's wealth and how it is generated. The human development measures the access the population has to wealth, jobs, education, nutrition, health, leisure and safety as well as political and cultural freedom. There is no single way to calculate the level of development because of the variety of economic indicators and the multiplicity of cultures and people. To assess the economic development of a country, economists use economic indicators including the Gross Domestic Product (GDP) which is the total value of goods and services produced by a country in a year; Gross National Product (GNP) which measures the total economic output of a country, including earnings from foreign investments and GNP per capita which is a country's GNP divided by its population. Economic growth measures the annual increase in GDP, GNP, GDP per capita, or GNP per capita.

## Good Governance

Good governance is described as how public institutions conduct public affairs and manage public resources.[2] Governance is "the process of decision-making and the process by which decisions are implemented (or not implemented)". The term governance can be applied to corporate, international, national, local governance or to interactions between other sectors of society. The concept centres on the responsibility of governments and the governing bodies to meet the needs of the masses as opposed to some selected groups in society. For the analysis of good governance one can look at any of the following relationships: between government and markets, between government and citizens, between government and the private or voluntary sector, and between elected officials and appointed officials. Three institutions can be reformed to promote good governance: the state, the private sector and the civil society. The main characteristics of good governance are accountability, transparency, respect of the rule of law, effectiveness and efficiency, and also that it should be participatory.

## Armed Forces

The Burmese military (better known as the *Tatmadow*) ruled the country outright for almost fifty years, and it retains considerable power even today. The army's allocation of 25 percent of seats in the Parliament enables it to veto any changes to the constitution in addition to retaining authority through the direct control of the ministries of Defence, Interior and Border, and have a majority in the powerful National Defence and Security Council—the country's most important executive body. If Burma is to continue to evolve into a free and democratic system, the civil–military relations must be fundamentally transformed. The immediate challenge is to create room for civilian involvement in security matters and eventually the military must accept the legitimacy and competency of civilian governments to direct and determine security policies.

Since 1962, active-duty military officers (and retired officers) have occupied most important positions in the central government and the military-business nexus has been found controlling investments in major natural resources sectors through the military-controlled enterprises like the Myanmar Economic Corporation (MEC) and the Union of Myanmar Economic Holdings Limited (UMEHL) or their sub-entities.[3]

There is no transparency relating to the revenues from the natural resources or where these revenues are ending up. According to many observers, the military must retreat from the day-to-day workings of the government. It must step back from active involvement in the economic and political activities towards acceptance of a proper civilian control. It must be reformed to uphold international human rights and humanitarian law, to evolve into a respected and an apolitical institution. Burma is in a period of transition from direct military rule to civilian control, but there is no guarantee that the political system will eventually be free from the military's interference. So, the reformers in Burma must cautiously and slowly work with the military to rearrange its duties and responsibilities while making deeper normative changes in the civilian–military relationship.

## Administration

The task of transforming the way the Burmese government operates and delivers services to the citizens should be a priority for the future government. Presently poor administration, ineffectual policymaking and weak structures of accountability remain as significant barriers to effective public service delivery in the country. Clearly, the most successful efforts to streamline public administration are rooted in a firm understanding of an organisation's statutory framework, its mandate, responsibilities, resources and existing ways of working. Public service delivery is rarely the responsibility of a single organisation. Local agencies must be responsible for implementing their service on ground; multiple ministries must be involved in planning and budgeting the policy directions.

No matter how efficient a central department is, bottlenecks will emerge if the local delivery bodies lack the capacity to deliver services, or if the centre lacks the authority to enforce the required changes in the ways they are expected to do so. But taking a sector-wide or government-wide approach to administrative reform is no small task; it requires the engagement of a wide range of stakeholders, from the political leadership to senior officials to regional and local managers. It also requires an effective diagnosis of real problems inhibiting service delivery, from skill shortages at different levels to the conflicting priorities or disconnected processes; from inadequate financial resources to an unclear policy mandate or an outdated legislative framework of power and duties.

Effective decision-making processes at the core of government are a prerequisite for a well-functioning public sector. The right management structures and processes can be established through careful analysis of the real underlying issues. Understanding and resolving these issues are not merely a technical matter, but will often require sensitivity to personalities, to process and to the political context. Building the capacity of the policy advisers, recommending reorganisation of the government structure to remove the overlapping responsibilities and supporting the introduction of new approaches to strategic planning and budgeting can be vital in improving Burma government's decision-making ability and in underpinning the administrative reform more widely.

## Parliament

In a fully democratic country like the United Kingdom, a functioning Parliament involves examining and challenging the work of the government and passing all laws.[4] Members of the Parliament debate the big political issues of the day and make proposals for new laws. The principal methods include questioning the government ministers and debating and investigating the work of the committees. In the UK, the Prime Minister and ministers from each government department attend the Parliament to answer oral questions. The Parliament is responsible for approving new laws (legislation). All debates are recorded in a publication which is available online or in print. The Parliament and government both play a part in forming the laws. Likewise, it is very important to have a functioning Parliament in Burma, which is an essential part of a flourishing democracy.

## Election

A country cannot be truly democratic until its citizens have the opportunity to choose their representatives through elections that are free and fair.[5] Free and fair elections[6] play a critical role in advancing democratisation and encouraging political liberalisation. Critical development efforts cannot succeed without a legitimate and democratically elected government that is responsive and accountable to its citizens. Elections provide an important opportunity to encourage political liberalisation. For free and fair elections, certain civil liberties like freedom of speech, association and assembly, are required. Electoral processes offer political parties and civic groups an opportunity to mobilise, organise supporters and share alternative platforms with the public. Elections also serve to encourage political debate and public dialogue. Fundamental electoral rights cannot be divorced from the election processes, procedures and institutions.

## Corruption

Besides elections, Burma also needs to alleviate corruption charges against its administrative organs. Corruption undermines democratic institutions, slackens economic development and contributes to governmental instability.[7] Literally, every sector of the government is dominated by cronies, especially in the booming extractive sector, where the profit margins are high. The active involvement of civil society, which includes

NGOs, community groups, labour unions, indigenous groups, charitable organisations, professional associations and foundations, is essential to help tackle corruption. Burma must endeavour to ensure that its public services are subject to safeguards that promote efficiency, transparency and recruitment based on merit.

Transparency and accountability in matters of public finance must be promoted. The state requires establishing criminal and other offences to cover wide range of illegal activities including corruption, bribery, embezzlement of public funds, influence in trading and laundering. To counter rampant corruption and red-tapism, measures should be taken to manage public revenues efficiently and limit the effects of the Dutch Disease.[8] Preventive measures include requiring the public officials to disclose earnings and assets, and stricter rules on the funding available to political parties and for electoral campaigns.

## Rule of Law

Under the previous junta regime, the legal system refrained from prohibiting arbitrary arrest or detention, and the government routinely employed both practices. The Myanmar Police Force, the Military Security Affairs (MSA) officers and Special Branch (SB) police officers were responsible for detaining persons suspected of "political crimes". There were no effective legal mechanisms available to investigate the security forces abuses. The judiciary was not independent of the government. The military appointed the judges to the Supreme Court, who in turn appointed the lower court judges with military approval. These courts adjudicated cases under the decrees promulgated by the military with the force of law. The legal system and its operation are seriously flawed; particularly, in the handling of political cases.

Strengthening the rule of law requires an independent judiciary. Burma needs judges and lawyers who are able to operate independently and impartially to provide proper jurisprudence.[9] Article 10 of the Universal Declaration of Human Rights says that everyone is entitled to a fair and public hearing by an independent and impartial tribunal. The United Nations General Assembly has for its part unanimously affirmed that 'human rights, the rule of law and democracy are interlinked and mutually reinforcing'. International laws and standards also state that governments must prioritise the provision of sufficient resources to ensure the judiciary's ability to provide independent and impartial tribunals. Burma's judiciary desperately needs these resources. Many courthouses lack the most basic facilities. At present, the judges in Burma do not have full access to the necessary cases, laws and international standards.

But, improving the independence of the judiciary and bolstering the rule of law requires systematic and concerted effort of the government and, in particular, from the powerful executive and legislative branches of the same. The executive and legislature must assist the judiciary to become a proper, equal branch of the government, able to regulate its own affairs and be accountable to the people's demands. It is crucial for the Burmese government to ensure that the judiciary is granted the independence and the resources necessary to improve the rule of law in the country. The task is daunting but this is the only way to strengthen the rule of law here.

## National Reconciliation and National Security

In order to achieve national reconciliation in Burma, peace between the government and the ethnic minorities is essential. At present, 14 major armed ethnic groups have signed ceasefire agreements with the government, but those agreements appear to be nothing more than a short-term fix that offers economic incentive through development projects. None of those agreements include concrete plan for political dialogue to address the underlying political, economic and social causes of the ongoing armed conflict in the ethnic regions. Sustaining peace in Burma needs a genuine political will from all sides. The Burmese government has refused to enter into a political dialogue with the ethnic armed groups, and instead, has demanded that the ethnic armies join the country's subordinate Border Guard Forces.

For the ethnic groups, the goal of political dialogue is to achieve equality as member states in the Union of Burma. The other challenging issues intertwined with these are those related to federalism, security reform, the return of Internally Displaced Persons (IDPs) and refugees who are largely members of ethnic minority groups, many of whom live in refugee camps in the neighbouring countries. National reconciliation will only be meaningful if all the key stakeholders are able to actively participate and make contributions at every level of the peace process. Participation of civil society organisations and concerned citizens is crucial for peacemaking and peace-building. So far, both the government and armed ethnic groups have only selectively or cautiously adhered to civil society initiatives, thus failing to capitalise on the existing potential for conflict resolutions.

Burma needs national security[10] which is not only focused on military might but also encompasses a broad range of facets all of which impinge on the non-military and on other values espoused by the society at large. Security threats involve not only conventional foes such as other nation-states but also non-state actors such as terrorist groups. Although national security measures are imposed to protect the society as a whole, many such measures may restrict the rights and freedom of individuals.

## Ethnic Issues

There are more than 135 different ethnic groups in Burma, each with its own history, culture and language. The majority Bamar group makes up about two-third of the population and controls the military and the government. The minority ethnic nationalities, making up the remaining one-third, live mainly in the resource-rich border areas and hills of Burma. The seven ethnic states make up approximately 60 percent of the national territory. Though ethnic groups generally have their own language and customs, Burmese remains the mandatory language of instruction in state schools, and teaching in local languages is not included in the curriculum. There are very few domestic publications in the indigenous minority languages.

Since 1948, the Panglong Agreement[11] has never been honoured and despite the fact that some smaller ethnic groups have demanded autonomy within larger ethnic states, the Burmese military government has refused to devolve power to the ethnic regions, arguing that doing so would lead to the breakup of the union. In addition, millions of people from these minority groups have become IDPs within Burma, or refugees in the neighbouring countries due to prolonged civil war.

Ethnic nationalities worry that they will continue to be marginalised if their concerns are not addressed in conjunction with the struggle for democracy. In support of their demand, the pro-democracy leader, Daw Aung San Suu Kyi, and the NLD have forged closer ties with the ethnic groups[12] while the Burmese government has urged armed ethnic opposition groups to accept ceasefires. These agreements have given the ethnic groups economic privileges and have allowed them to retain their arms. However, analysts note that most of these ceasefires are in nascent stages and have a long way to go. Ceasefires are only the beginning of a process of peace-building and national reconciliation. To move from ceasefires to national reconciliation and then to enable a political dialogue, the government has to deliver significant improvements in the daily lives of the people in the former conflict areas and also promote an adequate decentralisation of power in these areas.

## Buddhist Monks

Buddhism was adopted in Burma in the eleventh century and now about 90 percent of the Burmese people follow Theravada Buddhism.[13] The ancient Burmese kings had collected many treatises—particularly those written in Sanskrit—brought from India for the royal library and had encouraged their study and translated them into Burmese. They were keen enthusiasts who contributed immensely to the welfare of the *Sangha* (Monks' Community), peace, progress and prosperity of the religion. With the arrival of Buddhism, Burma underwent major changes in various aspects of its life including language, culture, art, literature and civilisation. This religion has played an important role in unifying the people of the country as it has brought the racial groups into one united whole under one religious banner.[14]

But, under the British government, Buddhism was not patronised by the colonial government and the Buddhist monks have always been at the forefront in their fight for an independent Burma as well as in the country's protests against the successive military regimes. But, the former military regime in power repressed these voices as they refused to allow the imprisoned monks to shave their heads or receive food in accordance with the monastic code. The Buddhist monks were beaten and forced into hard labour. The junta told the *Sangha* members to distance themselves from politics, political parties and members of the political parties. In addition, the Buddhist monks' rights to vote were ignored under the 2008 Constitution.[15]

## Strategies for Burma

Thus, for a successful re-engagement, Burma needs to implement comprehensive economic and political reforms characterised by a human-centric, sustainable, inclusive and balanced economic growth.

Effective and long-term human rights protection in Burma can be achieved by building a flourishing democratic system and rule of law. Democracy is necessary to ensure efficiency, transparency and accountability of the government. Democracy and rule of law, in turn, depend on a flourishing civil society, including an independent media, political parties, institutions and campaigns groups better represented by the NGOs, given the fact that a well-functioning civil society enables the citizens to question and analyse the government policies, which in turn would ensure that the government's actions are transparent and legitimate. In the absence of a functioning democracy in Burma, corruption and injustice will persist in the country. The protection of human rights depends on the establishment of democracy and respect for the rule of law, and they in turn depend on an active civil society. The UN Declaration on Human Rights in 1998 affirms the right of everyone to work for the protection of human rights. The pressure must be kept up on Burma to end all human rights abuses and to permit democracy.

## Poverty Alleviation and Sustainable Development

First, the process of gradual economic reforms must be initiated in Burma. Economic growth and building of an infrastructure are essential. The country should make use of trade liberalisation to make trade work positively for poverty reduction. To support its less-advantaged population, the Burmese government should initiate microfinance programmes. While high growth can be good for poverty reduction, broad-based and labour-utilising growth is even better. This type of pro-poor growth requires sound macroeconomic management and policies that encourage steady growth in employment. Good governance is extremely important for poverty reduction. It not only helps to establish sound macroeconomic management policies and ensure that these policies are implemented, but also enables the transparent use of public funds, encourages growth of the private sector, promotes an effective delivery of public services and helps to establish rule of law. Moreover, an equitable growth that promotes the welfare of the poor can be achieved only through an effective, progressive tax system and an adequate allocation for basic education, primary healthcare and other public services.

Public sector inefficiency and corruption leave insufficient resources for supporting public services and the targeted anti-poverty programmes. In this area, the incumbent government must provide microloans where small amounts of money are given out as loans to the farmers or villagers, who can then obtain physical capital to increase their economic rewards. Finally, social protection is another area that has received considerable attention for reducing poverty. Therefore, legislative reform, institution-building and support for legal assistance, access to justice, employment, reproductive health and environmental protection must be implemented. Cultural factors, such as discrimination of various kinds, can negatively affect productivity. Support for gender equality, and inclusion of marginalised groups within are the key to arrest poverty. To this, may be added the issue of 'sustainable development' which requires proper regulation and supervision of the financial sector aimed at protecting depositors, enhancing competition, increasing efficiency and expanding the availability of financial resources to all members of the society. In short, a sound macroeconomic system will require getting rid of "market-distorting interventions"—especially, the overvalued official exchange rates along with import and export licenses that restrict trade. Burma should encourage flourishing financial institutions that aim at collective development of the masses at large.

## Conclusion

Burma is thought to be on its path towards democratic transition. Only pragmatic leadership and good governance can give Burma its political and economic stability. The speed with which Burma would industrialise and attract Foreign Direct Investment (FDI) depends on how the country addresses its challenges. After more than half a century of brutal, debilitating military rule, the country is in the process of a calculated top-down course reversal, which has unleashed a bottom-up awakening of the political, economic and civil society activities.

Among the most urgent priorities are the resolution of ethnic and sectarian conflicts; creation of jobs for the vast majority of the population which lives in poverty; transformation of the role of the military; tackling corruption and establishing the rule of law. Engagement with Burma should be encouraged in order to counter China's influence over the country. Women's participation in every aspect of daily life should be promoted.

To use foreign trade as a major vehicle of growth, Burma should make every effort to expand road and railway network around the country through the creation of a network of expressways and railways and work effectively on its Special Economic Zones (SEZs). The country should set long-term goals of providing compulsory education from the elementary-school level to the middle-school level. Historically, the Burmese civilisation has been influenced by Buddhism which has played an important part in shaping its culture and lifestyle. This cultural consciousness, a sense of deep history and a largely inward-looking national perspective, can indirectly contribute to the growth of Burma's economy.

In order to promote other forms of economic reform, Burma needs to work on building up of rural enterprises and private businesses, liberalise foreign trade and investment, relax state control over some prices, and invest in industrial production and the education of its workforce. Here, market-oriented reforms should be undertaken which will be critical in creating the productivity boom. The reforms will raise the economic efficiency of private businesses, foreign investors and traders. As long as

Burma has plentiful supply of agricultural workers willing to work in factories, and as long as Burma remains the lowest-cost supplier of manufactured goods, it can continue to grow. By welcoming foreign investment, Burma's open-door policy will be adding power to its economic transformation. This foreign money will enable the country to build factories and create jobs, and ensure smooth transfer of technology. By encouraging the growth of rural enterprises and not focusing exclusively on the urban industrial sector, Burma can move millions of workers off farms and into factories without creating an urban crisis.

The Burmese government should allow foreign investors to manufacture and sell wide range of goods in the domestic market and authorise the establishment of Wholly Foreign-Owned Enterprises, which is now the preferred form of FDI. Most of Burma's financial institutions, owned and governed by the state, if effectively managed, can contribute to monitoring the cash flow, administering accounts, payments and receipts of government organisations and disbursing budgetary expenditures to the government's economic plans. The state can guide the country's economic development by making broad decisions on economic priorities and policies as well as the state budget. Gradually, Burma needs to rebalance its economy from the one that is driven by investment and exports to a more consumption-driven one since the growth in the economy can come from domestic consumption. Trade liberalisation can be economically beneficial to the country as integration into the world economy has proven a powerful tool for countries to promote economic growth, development and poverty reduction. Growth also improves public revenues. This enables the government to spend more on physical and social infrastructure, which in turn helps to reduce poverty and at the same time improve the country's productive potential. Good governance and active civilian participation play important roles in harnessing development. The presence of capital-abundant, high-tech TNCs in Burma could stifle the domestic industry that is still in its infancy.

Burma should shield some industries from overseas competition so that they can grow and compete with foreign flagships on a level-playing field. There is a desperate need to provide reliable electricity and internet connections, and to upgrade the country's antiquated roads and transports. Only with a sound infrastructure can both the local and foreign investors succeed. While the government is right to expand the education budget, it should also aim to improve the quality of education. Investment in education and infrastructure should ease the inflationary pressures and allow room for the central bank to lower the current punitive interest rates, which are as high as 13 percent. Lower interest rates will reduce the cost of borrowing for the domestic firms and spur investment. The authorities in Burma need to establish clear set of rules that favour nobody and this will take time. Press freedom is required to shed light on the unwanted state discretions and act as a check on the system.

Redefining and professionalising the military's political and economic roles are some of the most important actions which Burma needs to take. Until the military can be removed from dominating the country's economy, both political reconciliation with the minority nationalities and the economic development are likely to remain elusive. If the country's reform process fails to deliver, then dire poverty and instability will deter the overall development plans of the country. The military–business nexus is still strong despite political reforms. If Burma is to develop the political economy of a modern, rights-respecting democratic state, the government will have to tackle this nexus with the tools of transparency—auditing, public disclosure and full accountability for corruption. Burma needs to firmly establish the rule of law and strengthen the judicial branch.

The judicial branch remains a major weakness in the new government structure. This is partly a structural problem, and partly the result of long decades of judicial abuse practiced by successive military governments. An important element of strong democratic societies is adherence to the rule of law, which in turn depends on a strong constitution that has broad public support. The Burmese citizens have repeatedly called for changes to Burma's 2008 Constitution so that the document may better reflect the country's new democratic aspirations. Revision and repeal of flawed laws and regulations is another key area for the government to effectively work on. A number of laws remain in place; many are hangovers from the colonial administration that are inconsistent with the international human rights standards. While the government has mostly ceased enforcing these laws, reforming the outdated legal statutes should be a high priority for the Parliament and the executive.

Independence of the judiciary is also critical for advancing reforms. Improvements need to be made in the quality of legal education, training of legal professionals and investigators, accessibility of laws and electronic and forensic evidence. The Office of the High Commissioner for Human Rights can provide key technical assistance and training to the government and civil society actors to support the rule of law and legal reform. The government of Burma should sign and ratify the key human rights treaties. Although the reform process has opened the door to new freedoms over the past two years, they have not been enshrined legally.

Burma needs to develop effective formulas for ethnic equality. Political transition by itself is not enough to achieve ethnic equality; some hard, practical decisions about power-sharing—both political and economic, eventually necessitating a constitutional amendment—will be required. Development of a serious debate over how to define federalism in Burma, and efforts to strengthen local government, decentralise the administrative authority at the federal level, are important steps. Burma needs to instill social and religious tolerance. Communal violence occurring between the Buddhist and Muslim populations is providing a fertile ground for the small bands of troublemakers to turn local disputes into major conflicts. The civil police must be properly organised and trained to prevent and respond effectively to mob violence. At the same time, the civil society, the religious and government leaders must address intolerance and prejudice urgently through sustained education and counselling.

Corruption is endemic to Burma's government and economy presents one of the most serious challenges to the reform process, democratization and economic liberalisation. Burma must address the "missing middle"—a capacity void across the spectrum of the government and the economy. The 'missing middle', where the reforms should be translated from policy into practice, is not empowered and lacks the capacity to engage in the work needed to address these issues and to implement solutions. Burma needs to deliver the benefits of reforms to the broader population. The government must encourage and direct the investment towards job creation and agriculture that empowers the ordinary farmers and not the crony class, to seek the benefits of a flourishing economic system.

Regarding land and property rights, the people in Burma are still being unfairly displaced by large business and agricultural projects without any adequate compensation or the means of providing a livelihood. Here, new models must be introduced for ensuring that local residents gain a fair share in the large development projects and that they have stable land rights that cannot be arbitrarily removed. Burma needs to develop mechanisms for negotiating trade-offs between economic development on the one hand, and social development and environmental protection on the other. As investment in Burma grows, it will be essential to work with the local communities affected by the development projects in order to address their needs and to avoid having popular protests seriously impeding the country's economic development and construction of an essential national infrastructure.

In the ethnic-minority areas, it will be necessary to ensure that proceeds from the large resource extraction projects are shared fairly with the local populace. Macroeconomic stabilisation and new investment laws are major steps towards improving the business environment for foreign investors. The lack of access to a fair justice system leaves people with no means to redress their grievance of displacement. Transitions are never smooth, and it is likely that the situation on the ground in Burma will get messier before it gets better. The reform process has opened an important and as yet unprecedented political space. But, an open political space will not bring a meaningful change unless more people throughout the country and in all segments of the society move into this space and start to use it.

Making Burma a home for its people will require broad grassroots engagement by the widest possible range of its citizens, from ethnic leaders and bloggers, to lawyers and lawmakers, to factory workers and human rights advocates. All of these groups will need to push for structural changes from the bottom up, while at the same time the political leadership works to push reform from the top down. Where these two forces would meet is up to the Burmese to build trust on both sides and to negotiate a space where they can coexist peacefully. In conclusion, it would be apt to articulate that the processes of democratisation, development and poverty reduction in Burma are interrelated and interdependent on each other, requiring concerted effort of everyone.

## NOTES

1. Characteristics of Democracy, http//iipdigital.usembassy.gov/st/English/publication/2008
2. http://www.unescap.org/resources/what-good-governance.
3. http://www.state.gov/e/eb/rls/othr/ics/2013/204612.htm.
4. http://dictionary.reference.com/browse/parliament.
5. http://www.usaid.gov/what-we-do/democracy/democracy-human rights-governance/supporting free-and-fair elections.
6. http://osce.usmission.gov/statements/free-and-fair elections 2/
7. http://www.unodc.org/unodc/en/corruption/
8. The negative consequences arising from a large increase in a country's income. The Dutch Disease is primarily associated with a natural resource discovery, but it can result from any large increase in foreign currency, including foreign direct investment, foreign aid or a substantial increase in the natural resource prices. http://www.investopedia.com/terms/dutchdisease.asp
9. http://www.dvb.no/analysis/making-rule-of-law-a-reality-in-myanmar-burma/37387.
10. In 2010, the White House included an all-encompassing worldview in a national security strategy which identified "security" as one of the country's "four enduring national interests" that were "inexorably intertwined".
11. http://www.blc-burma.org/?q=node/136.

12. http://www.elevenmyanmar.com/index.php?option=com_content&view=article&id=6794.
13. http://bdcburma.wordpress.com/budhism/
14. http://bdcburma.wordpress.com/2013/09/02
15. http://www.blc-burma.org/sites/default/files/Analysis%20on%20SPDC's%202008%20Constitution.pdf

# 2

# Myanmar's Political Landscape: A Profile

*Khin Maung Win*

Following the general elections held in 2010, a new civilian government was sworn in on 30 March 2011, bringing an end to more than two decades of direct military rule. At the same time, it was no surprise that many observers from the international community as well as local politicians had looked at the 2010 elections and the new government with a sense of scepticism, particularly as the elections were held under the 2008 Constitution of the Republic of the Union of Myanmar, written under the guidance of the military regime, giving special privileges and powers to the military. The fact that the post of the President, the head of the executive branch, was held by the same person who had been the Prime Minister in the previous military government and that many of the top posts in the new set up, including most of the ministers, the Speakers of both the legislative organs, were also held by former generals or high-ranking military officers, naturally gave credence that the new government was no more than a continuation of the former regime in a civilian cloak. In other words, as one commentator puts it, "old wine in new bottle".

But, the actual events of the past four years have confounded these views. It is now generally accepted that fundamental changes and reforms have taken place. As President U Thein Sein himself had declared, Myanmar is still in a state of transition and in his New Year address on 1 January 2015, the President stated: "...we understand we still have a long way to go before we can get to our destination. It is likely that we will not always be able to meet all the public expectations when we have to undertake several reforms concurrently."[1]

## Paving the Way

Speaking to the members of his government on 10 June 2014, President U Thein Sein said that his government had instituted reforms through systematic measures which he termed as "reform wave". He declared, "the first wave of reforms dealt with the introduction of a multiparty democratic system and the transition from the old to a new system, while the second wave of reforms puts emphasis on strategies for executive, economic, political and social up gradation."[2] He added that the third wave that is being implemented would concentrate on "ensuring a solid foundation for a new democracy to take root and a higher living standard for people."[3]

Indeed, the reforms have touched every aspect of life in the nation, from political conditions to economic and social spheres. It is generally acknowledged that the political landscape has changed dramatically since the new government was installed in 2011. The political parties, including the National League for Democracy (NLD) led by Daw Aung San Suu Kyi, are playing a very active and dynamic role in the political process.

Under the present Constitution, the highest legislative organ is the *Pyidaungsu Hluttaw* comprising of the *Pyi Thu Hluttaw* and the *Amyothar Hluttaw*. The developments in the last four years have clearly shown that assemblies are not rubber-stamp institutions as they have taken action and made proposals that are not exactly in tune with the government. According to the International Crisis Group:

> "Myanmar's new legislature, the Union Assembly (*Pyidaungsu Hluttaw*) formed in 2011 on the basis of elections the previous year, has turned out to be far more vibrant and influential than expected. Both its lower and upper houses have a key role in driving the transition process through the enactment and amendment of legislation needed to reform the outdated legal code and are acting as a real check on the power of the executive."[4]

Likewise, the judiciary is also undertaking measures to make itself more independent and to stamp out corruption. Media censorship has ended and there is a blossoming of private newspapers, weekly journals and magazines. Moreover, the emergence of civil society organisations is a reflection of this new found freedom. President U Thein Sein rightly pointed out, "Some recent surveys indicate that ordinary citizens can now enjoy more freedom, namely in the area of freedom of expression, and that citizens in most parts of the country noted that they do not have to live in constant fear due to the political and administrative reforms undertaken in 2014 and earlier."[5]

The transformation that is taking place in Myanmar was also recognised by foreign governments, scholars and media. Enumerating the changes that had taken place in recent years, Ms Priscilla Clapp, former US Charge d Affaires at the US Embassy in Yangon from 1999 to 2002 and currently working at the Asia Society, wrote:

> Whereas the previous military regime turned a blind eye and deaf ear to human rights, democracy, and good economic governance, the new government, has sought to open its society, introduce freedom of information and association, which were previously strictly denied, reconcile with the democratic opposition and ethnic armed organisations, and develop a government structure capable of reflecting the full diversity of its society. It has – at least in aspiration, if not yet in practice – embraced the fundamental values of liberal democracy as its goal. While there is still a long road ahead, with continued military control of essential political and economic sectors as a major roadblock, a course has been set and there has been sufficient progress to make an about face extremely costly, because this would certainly cause a steep decline in foreign investment and assistance. Although still far from meeting its goals, the transition's record of achievement is impressive, but it has also exposed the depth of the problems confronting the country's reformers.[6]

Likewise, the US President Barack Obama, in his remarks to President U Thein Sein in Naypyitaw on 13 November 2014, said:

> "In part because of President Sein's leadership, the democratisation process in Myanmar is real and we can point to specific changes that are making the difference. Domestically, we've seen political prisoners have been released. We have seen an effort to end the practice of children being recruited into the army. There is a genuine prospect for a ceasefire between some of the armed groups that have been fighting in Myanmar for decades.
>
> But in our discussions, we recognised that this process is still incomplete. So, specifically, we had the opportunity to discuss elections that are scheduled for next year and the need for those elections to be fair, inclusive, transparent, and the constitutional amendment process that has begun needs to reflect the ability of all voices in Myanmar's society to participate."

He also went on to add: "So we recognise that change is hard, and that it doesn't always move in a straight line, but I am optimistic about the possibilities in Myanmar."[7]

Thus, it has been generally acknowledged by the people and the international community that there had been genuine fundamental reforms and changes in the nation since the new government under President U Thein Sein took power. Indeed, these changes are evident in the political atmosphere of the nation with the people being able and willing to take part in the political process of the country and equally willing to express their views and opinions freely. The newly founded freedom in the country has indeed been exhilarating.

## Issues and Challenges

While the reform movement has swept over the country during the last four years of the new government, the nation still faces many issues and challenges—issues inherited from history as well as challenges that had grown out of the changes themselves. The success in meeting and overcoming these difficult and complex issues will surely have a great impact on the country and its people.

Transitions from one political system to another are seldom smooth and easy. Indeed, there are instances where the transition to democracy has failed and where nations have either reverted back to direct or indirect military rule or fallen into a state of anarchy and bloodshed. It is noteworthy that the present transition in Myanmar has been relatively smooth. But this does not mean that it is free from problems and challenges.

On 31 October 2014 President U Thein Sein during his meeting with the Speakers of both legislative organs, the Comander-in-Chief of Defence Services Senior General Min Aung Hlain, heads of major political parties including Daw Aung San Suu Kyi candidly identified the various challenges faced by the government. At the meeting, the President enumerated the challenges, saying "...the challenges that we will have to overcome include: state building; socio-economic reforms; development of a democratic culture; national reconciliation based on the peace process; and democratic governance including rule of law."[8]

Out of the many challenges facing the nation, the issue of bringing peace to the nation is the most important requirement as peace is directly linked to the progress and prosperity of the nation. The insurgency problem emerged soon after Myanmar's independence in 1948, making it one of the longest in the world. Various governments since then have tried to tackle the issue in various fashions but still it continues to fester. As this issue is of utmost importance for peace and development of the nation, the present government is also paying due attention to it. The Myanmar President in his radio address to the nation on 1 January 2015 rightly stated:

> "As many of you know, there are political stakeholders that have formed political parties within the framework of the 2008 Constitution to contest in the upcoming elections. In addition, there are armed factions who resorted to various armed struggles to resolve their own political disagreements. You will also notice at this time that many of these armed organisations are actively engaging in the peace process to find political solutions to these disagreements and settle their past grievances politically. In this way, the political process that we see today is shaped by avenues and opportunities for all political stakeholders to take part in. In the near future, I am hopeful that even the armed political groups will have an opportunity through the political dialogue process to participate in the political process directly."[9]

The peace talks have made considerable progress but some issues still remain unresolved. The government had hoped to sign a nationwide ceasefire early this year, but this objective proved to be too optimistic. However, one major difference from the peace efforts of the previous military government is that the present government is working not only to achieve a ceasefire but also to get engaged in political dialogue and find a political solution in order to resolve the issue.

The issue of national reconciliation with the ethnic races provides the foundation on which the peace process must be built. One of the major demands of the ethnic groups is for more autonomy in running the affairs of their respective areas. Although it used to be a dirty word during the time of the military government, today the concept of federalism has been accepted by the present government. President U Thein Sein reassured that "I am convinced that we will be able to establish a Federal Union on the basis of the agreements we will reach at the political dialogue."[10] The need to establish a form of federal system is shared by all the political stakeholders. Indeed, a federal form of government has been the consistent demand of the armed groups. Thus, it can be surmised that the present negotiations between the government and the armed groups would eventually lead to the amendment of the Constitution that would result in a federal system.

Another burning political issue is the question of amending the 2008 Constitution of the Union of Myanmar. The Constitution was drafted under the guidance of the then military government and contains articles which the NLD and other politicians would like to see amended. The NLD was able to obtain 5 million signatures towards amending the Constitution. The NLD's:

> "main focus is on changing Article 436 of the military-drafted constitution, which requires more than three-quarter of the Parliament votes to approve any amendments. Since the constitution upholds quarter of the seats in the lower house for military candidates, and another half by the military-backed, ruling Union Solidarity and Development Party (USDP), Article 436 effectively gives the Myanmar military a de facto veto over any changes. The NLD also hopes to alter Article 59(f), which bars any candidate from the presidency whose spouse, children, or parents, are foreign citizens, barring Suu Kyi from holding the nation's top office. (The NLD leader's children, like her late husband Michael Aris, are British citizens)".[11]

When the US came out with a statement saying "We believe that constitutional reform should pave the way for the Burmese to freely choose their President in a free and fair 2015 election", the government spokesperson U Ye Htut (who is now the Information Minister) retorted: "It is not the concern of the United States. It is inappropriate for us to tell how the US should amend their constitution and likewise the US should not dictate how it should be amended."[12] It is generally agreed that the chances of amending the Constitution before the 2015 elections are slim.

With regard to the current state of reforms, the NLD issued a statement on 13 January 2015 following the second meeting between the government, the Speakers of both the houses of Parliament, the Commander-in-Chief of Defence Services, the major political parties and the ethnic leaders the day before. The NLD statement criticised the government for:

- the lack of desire within the government to push reforms forward and to amend the Constitution;
- failing to protect individual human rights;
- failing to bring sustainable development to Myanmar's rural population;
- continuing its endeavours for centralisation;
- failing to cooperate fully with the parliament; and
- not arranging a six-party talk in accordance with the vote of the Union parliament.

The statement went on to stress the need for free and fair elections later this year by saying that: "The government needs to stay away from bias and ensure free and fair elections.

The Union Election Commission is required to stop the behavior that is not (in) conformity with rules and regulations. The administrative sector needs to avoid favouritism of political parties."[13]

Another important issue is the question of land disputes. During the previous military government, the state had confiscated large areas of land owned by large business enterprises popularly known as "cronies" i.e. people close to the previous government and the military. Addressing this issue, President U Thein Sein stated:

> "The land issue is one of the major challenges facing our country. The fact of the matter is that land reforms are never easy in any country; they are particularly difficult in transitional countries like ours. The land problems we are now left to deal with were caused by unnecessarily complicated procedures practiced by the previous governments and problems relating to documentation and record of ownership. In addition, questionable allocation of land to business projects by taking advantage of the existing loopholes in archaic land laws and doing so without proper public consultation has also led to land problems in the country.... I would like to note that the Union Government, after drawing lessons from dealing with the land issues in the past years, will do its utmost to undertake land reforms effectively and to help citizens regain ownership of the land they deserve."[14]

A case in point is the land dispute at the Letpadaungtaung area, where a joint venture company comprising a Chinese company and a military-owned enterprise is trying to develop a vast copper mine. Indeed, disturbances in the area have led to death and injury to the protesters of the project. The fact that land prices all over the nation have skyrocketed in the recent years has also contributed to the problem.

The nation also faces the issue of tension in the Rakhine state between the native Rakhine nationals and the Bengalis or Rohingyas (a term rejected by the Myanmar government). This has led to some incidents resulting in death and injury. As a result, over 100,000 Bengalis are living in refugee camps. The government is trying to solve the issue but the situation remains complex. Speaking on the government's attempt to solve the situation, President U Thein Sein said that his government is "currently finalising the Action Plan for Rakhine State. This plan is designed to bring social harmony between different communities and promote development in the state. The action plan will be implemented in consultation with the residents of the state and our international development partners."[15] The issue in hand is delicate and have been complicated by high emotions on both sides.

Another equally pressing issue, as expressed by the students through demonstration is to amend the Education Bill recently submitted by the government and passed by the Parliament. The students are demanding the right to form student unions, for more autonomy to the educational institutions and an increase in budget allocation to the education sector. A four-party negotiation consisting of the representatives of the government, the Parliament, the National Network for Education Reform and the students took place in Yangon early this year although there was a general agreement on the demands by the students, the situation remains delicate and complex.

Some observers and politicians, while acknowledging that there have been many positive changes in the country, have voiced their sense of anxiety at what they perceived as the slowing down or even some backtracking of the reforms. There is no doubt that the initial pace of reforms has been quite remarkable. But it must be realised that Myanmar, like many other developing countries, has its own set of issues and problems that pose a challenge to rapid change. Still, in spite of issues and difficulties, it would be wrong to say that the reform movement has been derailed. It is more of a reality check. As Mr Trevor Wilson, the former Australian Ambassador to Myanmar and currently with the Australian National University, wrote:

> "Myanmar's initial reforms beginning in March 2011 were dramatic and surprised everyone, but they are still incomplete and not always operating well. Many problem areas have not yet undergone reform (such as land reforms, judicial system reform, and ending human rights abuses), meaning that much 'unfinished business' remains. But this does not mean that Myanmar's reform process has stalled. ... The pace of reform in Myanmar has certainly slowed, but whether or not this is the result of a reduced commitment to reform calls for a considered, not just a politically oriented, assessment. To say that nothing much in the way of major reform happened during 2013–14 is not accurate..... While some reforms are undoubtedly not working as well as they should, or even as intended, reforms already undertaken have not simply been 'cosmetic' or 'symbolic'. They are reforms that are helping to change once and for all the constricting mindset of the last 50 years in Myanmar."[16]

## 2015: A Critical Year

According to the 2008 Constitution, the term of office for the executive, legislative and judicial organs is five years. Thus, the term of the current office bearers will come to an end in March 2016. As announced by the

Election Commission, the elections will take place either at the end of October or the beginning of November 2015. It is only natural that the political tempo is rising in the nation as various parties have started preparing for the forthcoming event.

President U Thein Sein remarked that "The year 2015 is crucial for Myanmar's democratic transition."[17] Identifying the tasks of his government for this year, he added that his government would "continue to strive to the best of its ability to consolidate the democratic reform program and bring the peace process to fruition, and to stand by our pledge to hold free and fair elections in 2015."[18]

Likewise, as the Chairperson of the NLD Daw Aung San Suu Kyi said: "The world knows that the year 2015 will be a very important year for our country. The most important thing is that the people make right decisions this year, I told a reporter recently. The decisions made this year will not affect this year alone; they will affect the country's future."[19]

Commenting on the issues facing the nation in 2015, Ms Priscilla Clapp said:

> "The coming year (2015) will provide a litmus test for the transition. The first question will be whether the ceasefire negotiations can produce an agreement allowing the ethnic armed groups and their supporters to participate in the political process. The second question will be whether the Parliament will vote to amend the constitution, diminishing those provisions that give the military a stranglehold over the democratic process. The third question will be whether the government can conduct free and fair elections in an atmosphere of relative security. The fourth question will be whether the body politic that emerges from the elections can reach consensus on new leadership in 2016 when the Parliament must choose the President, because, if conducted fairly, the elections are likely to produce relative parity among three major political groups: one bloc comprising the government USDP plus military representatives in Parliament, a second comprising the NLD and other democratic parties, and a third made up of the ethnic minority parties. The Parliament will look very different than it does today and coalition building will be essential. With these elections, therefore, Myanmar's transition will enter a critical new phase."[20]

Thus, the most important event of 2015 will be the general elections to be held later this year. The two biggest contenders will be the NLD and the ruling USDP. The NLD and its popular leader Daw Aung San Suu Kyi are expected to do well. However, it cannot be said with certainty that the party will enjoy the needed majority. In the areas where the ethnic races live, the ethnic political parties have certain advantages and the local people can be expected to vote along ethnic lines. Thus, given the organisation and financial strength of the USDP and the growing impact of the smaller parties, especially the ethnic-based parties, NLD may not enjoy the overwhelming success that it enjoyed during the 2012 by-elections.

Touching on the prospects of 2015, Daw Moe Thuzar from the Institute of South East Asian Studies rightly pointed out:

> The April 2012 by-elections suggest a future political scene dominated by two large parties: the USDP and the NLD... For the present, the NLD is the only political party – in terms of size and reach – capable of putting into place a viable alternative (such as a shadow cabinet) to the present government. Whether, in the 2015 general elections, the NLD can pursue this option singly or in a coalition remains to be seen. This is the primary challenge the opposition faces in the run-up to the 2015 general elections. While many hope that 2015 will usher in a new era of liberal democracy for Myanmar with the NLD at the helm, 2015 may not provide a sufficient timeline for opposition parties – large and small – to master the necessary resources to dislodge the USDP in Parliament.[21]

Until the Constitution is amended, the *Tatmadaw* (military) will continue to play an important role in national politics since it continues to hold 25 percent of the seats in the Parliament. The Commander-in-Chief of the Defence Services, Senior General Min Aung Hlaing, speaking on the role of the *Tatmadaw*, stated: "It's been only four years. We are still a young democracy. When we are moving towards a multi-party democratic system it needs to be a strong system. The military representatives in Parliament only give advice to the legislative process. They can never make decisions." With respect to the calls for amending the Constitution, he said, "It will depend a lot on the country's unity, its peace and stability. To specify an exact time is difficult." When asked whether he intends to run for Presidency, he demurred by saying that: "About becoming President, I will decide, depending on the situation of the times. If I turn my attention to (politics) now, it is likely to weaken the job I'm doing. Right now it is too early to make a decision and talk about it."[22]

Dr Nicholas Farrelly rightly observed: "Still, there's a good chance that Myanmar could muddle through 2015. Perhaps a new political compact could emerge, fusing the interests of democrats, conservatives, militarists and sub-nationalists. With negotiation, compromise and conciliation, some of Myanmar's rolling tragedies could be consigned to history."[23]

The question is not whether there will be political changes but rather how far these changes will be. It is also possible that because of the rising expectations of the people, there will be some sections who are not going to be satisfied with the pace of reforms. Hopefully, the issues of civil conflict, ethnic and other tensions will not derail the programme for reforms. Myanmar has many problems and challenges, but with the commitment of the government along with that of all stakeholders momentum for reforms, it can be surmised that:

- Myanmar will continue on the path of transition to a democratic state;
- The process will not always be easy and smooth;
- But there will be no turning back from this path;
- The 2015 elections could result in a new political landscape;
- Whatever government takes over in 2016, it will also inherit some difficult issues and challenges; and
- On the whole, foundations for a peaceful, stable and prosperous democracy are being laid down and there is a sense of hope and optimism about the future of the country.

## NOTES

1. *Global New Light of Myanmar*, 1-1-2015.
2. *Global New Light of Myanmar*, 11-6-2014.
3. Ibid.
4. Anonymous, "Not a Rubber Stamp: Myanmar's Legislature in a Time of Transition", *Asia Briefing*, No.142, 13 December 2013.
5. *Global New Light of Myanmar*, 1-1-2015
6. Priscilla Clapp, "Taking the Long View", *Asia Pacific Bulletin*, No.286, 10 November, 2014.
7. Remarks of the US President Barack Obama after the Bilateral Meeting with President Thein Sein of Burma, US Embassy Yangon, 13 November 2014.
8. *Global New Light of Myanmar*, 1-11-2014.
9. *Global New Light of Myanmar*, 1-1-2015.
10. *Global New Light of Myanmar*, 14-2-2015.
11. Sebastian Strangio, "Myanmar's Constitutional Uncertainty, *The Diplomat*, 21 July 2014.
12. "Myanmar Rejects US Call on Constitutional Reform", *The Associated Press*, 17 June, 2014.
13. "NLD Issues Statement Demanding Progress in Political Reforms", *The Nation*, 13 January 2015.
14. *Global New Light of Myanmar*, 1-1-2015.
15. Ibid.
16. Trevor Wilson, "Are Myanmar Reforms Stalled?" *ANU, East Asia Forum*, 1 February 2015.

17. President Thein Sein's New Year Day Message, 1 January 2015.
18. Ibid.
19. Daw Aung San Suu Kyi, "2015 will Determine the Country's Future", *D-Wave Journal*, 6 January 2015.
20. Priscilla Clapp, "Taking the Long View", *Asia Pacific Bulletin*, No.286, 10 November, 2014.
21. Moe Thuzar, "The 2012 By-Elections and the Future of Political Parties in Myanmar." (the Source is missing)
22. Interview with *Channel News Asia*.
23. Nicholas Farrelly, "The Myanmar Story doesn't End Here", *East Asia Forum*, 29 December 2014.

# 3

# General Elections, Peace Process of Myanmar and their Implications

*U Hla Myint*

To understand the implications of the 2015 general elections and the peace process, it is important to take a brief look at the last four years of President Thein Sein's government. Myanmar held its first parliamentary elections in 2010 after 20 years being under the military rule and the present government was sworn in on 30 March 2011. Since then, despite various criticisms of the results of the 2010 elections, the government has been engaged in domestic reform measures in various fields to establish democracy and to integrate Myanmar within the international community. Having seen the positive and dramatic changes as a result of those measures, the international community has begun to recognise, encourage and support the reforms in Myanmar. The most remarkable was the release of Daw Aung San Suu Kyi and other political prisoners, including the well-known figures like Min Ko Naing and Ko Ko Gyi and finally the victory of the National League for Democracy (NLD) in the 2012 by-elections, which led to the easing of sanctions by the United States and the European Union. It is imperative for Myanmar to establish peace and effectively manage the transition to maintain this confidence of the international community which is closely watching the events in the country and how the overall situation evolves. During his recent visit in February 2015, the global Director of Operations for the European Commission's Humanitarian Aid and Civil Protection Department (ECHO) stated that while they stand committed to contribute to addressing the humanitarian needs of the ethnic communities and minorities of the country, they will of course follow the situation through 2015. This remark reflects the general sentiments of the international community on the developments in Myanmar.

## The 2015 Elections

The upcoming 2015 elections and the peace process are the two most important events that have received the attention of the international community. There have been many speculations about the possible outcomes of these two events, which will influence the direction of democratisation and the success of the present government's developmental efforts. The failure to hold a free and fair election as scheduled and the lack of progress in the peace process towards the envisaged political dialogue may undermine the trust of the international community, which is essential for maintaining the momentum of the reform process. The positive reaction of the United States and the EU to the results of the 2012 by-elections is very illustrative in this regard. The importance of the peace process was emphasised by President U Thein Sein when he said in his broadcast speech on 1 October 2014: "if the ceasefire is not signed and political dialogue cannot start, the chance of political stability, transition and a general election in 2015 will be very slim." This remark understandably raised doubts about the upcoming elections as to whether it will be held or not as planned. But the remark cannot be lightly construed as indicating the possible postponement of the election. The President , it seems intended to highlight the important linkage between these two events and the interdependence that will have an impact on the current democratisation process. The Union Election Commission, however, announced subsequently that the election will be held by the end-October or early November 2015. Therefore, the Commission is in full-swing preparation for the election. It is in the process of preparing the national voting list and it will be completed in 330 townships across the country in July this year. The general public will have 14 days to check the list for any incorrect inclusions or exclusions. The Chairman U Tin Aye himself is on a tour of the country, meeting the members of the election sub-commissions and the relevant local authorities to ensure the successful holding of the election freely and fairly. Moreover, he has been receiving foreign organisations to inform them of the strenuous efforts being made by the Commission.

## The NLD's Position

About 70 political parties are expected to contest the elections, including the National League for Democracy (NLD). The NLD had boycotted the 2010 national elections but re-registered as a political party and competed in the by-elections in April 2012, winning 43 out of the 46 constituencies. Daw Aung San Suu Kyi represented the NLD in the township of Kawhmu in Yangon, easily winning a seat in the Lower House (*Pyithu Hluttaw*). At its Congress in December 2014, the NLD announced its intention to campaign vigorously for the 2015 general elections, while maintaining its efforts for constitutional reform. The party has focused on a year-long campaign aimed at amending the 2008 Constitution, because Article 436 of the Constitution allows the military an effective veto power over any constitutional reform. The administration affirms that the Constitution shall be amended with prior approval of more than seventy-five percent of all the representatives of the *Pyidaungsu Hluttaw*, followed by a nation-wide referendum of more than half of those who are eligible to vote. The Constitution bars Daw Aung San Suu Kyi, whose late husband had and two sons have British citizenship from running for the Presidency or Vice-Presidency due to Article 59(f).

Previously, the NLD had held a large number of public rallies at various cities where five million signatures were received in support of amendment to the Constitution. However, in mid-June, 2014 a 31-member Parliamentary committee, charged with exploring changes to the Constitution voted against amending Article 59(f). But, there have been unconfirmed reports that the Committee is open to changing Article 436. Rumours have it that the NLD may have agreed to forgo one for the other, but the details about the change have not yet been clearly disclosed. President U Thein Sein, in his monthly speech to the nation on 2 February 2015, referred to his stance on the amendment of the Constitution, asserting that the Constitution shall be amended under the right conditions and at the appropriate time for the benefit of the nation. He also added that some of the proposed amendments may require the electorate to decide in referendums, and the amendment process should follow the procedures set forth in the Constitution (GNLM dt 33-2-2015). In view of the positions of the Government and the Parliament, it is highly unlikely that the process for amendment of the said two articles will start before the 2015 elections. Furthermore, there remains only eight working months during which the Union Election Commission will be completely preoccupied with the preparations for the elections. If certain amendments require referendums, as pointed out by the President, it is practically impossible to engage in such a formidable exercise while the elections are so close.

## Possible Candidates for the Presidency in the 2015 Elections

With regard to the amendment of the Constitution, there are widespread speculations about the likely candidates for the Presidency. According to current news reports the incumbent President, the Speaker of the Lower House, the Commander-in-Chief of the Armed Forces and Daw Aung San Suu Kyi could be the possible contestants for the Presidency. Some reports even mention the General Secretary of the Union Solidarity and Development Party as a likely candidate. The President has already announced his intention not to run for the Presidency again in the 2015 elections. Nevertheless, considering his popularity with the people of Myanmar and the international community, his remarkable achievements in the reform process within a short span of time and encouragement to economic development with the forecasts of continued growth in the future, his candidacy cannot be ruled out. Because if there emerges a popular demand for his Presidency, the President might change his previous intention. If he becomes the President for the second term, the current momentum of democratisation will certainly continue and the international community will be more comfortable with its engagements with Myanmar in various areas.

The Chairman of the Lower House has clearly announced his intention to run for the Presidency and appears to be determined to strive for the post. He has been receiving all the foreign dignitaries coming to Myanmar on official visits after they have met officials from the government side and at the same time touring the country and meeting people in different constituencies. As the Chairman of the ruling Union Solidarity and Development Party (USDP), his candidacy is also promising and as someone who was in the third position of the previous government, he is a well-known figure. If the incumbent President decides not to run, he has a better chance, compared to the other contestants. As Chair of the Lower House, he has achieved much progress in the legislation field, by amending laws, repealing outdated laws and enacting many new laws. Because of his effective leadership at the Parliament (he is also the Speaker of the Union Parliament, *Pyidaung Su Hluttaw*), he may be elected President. Representing the same party, he is likely to maintain the current momentum of democratisation though slight changes in the approach may be anticipated. The international community may not find it difficult to work with him unless he follows an entirely different approach. However, there may be no obvious changes in the Myanmarese political landscape under the Presidency of the Speaker of the Lower House.

Despite the obstacles in her attempts to amend the Constitution, according to the news reports, Daw Aung San Suu Kyi is constantly striving to have the two articles amended during the remaining months. Regardless of whether the Constitution is amended or not, the NLD will contest the elections this year. If the result of the 2012 by-election is something to judge by, the NLD is likely to win more seats in the Parliament this time. With the increased number of representatives, the NLD's political clout is expected to grow stronger. This scenario is not possible if the 2015 elections are not free and fair. Therefore, there have been calls for and expressions of concern about a free and fair election. The importance of a free and fair election is fully appreciated by the President and in his New Year message, he had reiterated his pledge to hold free and fair polls this year. In this regard, he had called for cooperation and support not only from the administration, but also from the security forces, political parties, civil society and the general public. He characterised the 2015 elections as one of the most critical steps in the democratic transition process of Myanmar. In view of these pledges coming from the highest political levels, the 2015 elections are expected to be free and fair, although some irregularities may be likely in some constituencies.

The candidacy of the Commander-in-Chief is doubted because there has been no confirmation in this regard from any quarter. The fact that he is nearing the retirement age had caused speculations about his possible candidacy in the first place. Because of the elections, 2015 has been dubbed as the make or break year for Myanmar. While the successful holding of the elections will certainly bring more investment, more businesses and more assistance into the country, an unfair election may lead to dire consequences like reduction or suspension of investment or even tightening of the remaining sanctions. Being aware of these consequences, the President and the Commission are keeping no stones unturned for ensuring a secure environment in Myanmar. At the same time, the *Pyidaungsu Hluttaw* is considering a national referendum bill and is debating the question of voting rights. People in the far-flung areas of Myanmar do not have national identification cards, which are required for voting. Due to the difficulties in the citizenship scrutinising process, in order to rectify this situation, the President has announced that the holders of temporary identification documents can vote. There were differences in the debate at the *Pyidaungsu Hlutta* over the President's announcement and the result of the debate was not conclusive. According to one of the Members of Parliament participating in the debate, nearly

1.5 million people will lose their voting rights unless the issue is resolved. Because of the controversy over the issue, the President's Office has issued a notification, according to which the holders of temporary cards are now required to surrender their cards and will be scrutinised in accordance with the relevant laws, rules and regulations.

Another issue of importance faced by the election process is the voting system. The election in 2010 was held following the First Past the Post (FPTP) system, under which the winning candidate in each and every constituency wins that seat in the Parliament. Daw Aung San Suu Kyi who won the constituency of Kawhmu won that seat in the Lower House. Now there have been calls for the introduction of the Proportional Representation (PR) System. This system offers each contesting party a proportional number of seats in the Parliament to the total number of votes that the party's candidates have received. There are both supporters for and opponents to the introduction of this PR System. An Electoral Review Commission (ERC) was set up to review the voting systems and to make recommendations on the suitability of various systems for the 2015 elections. The Lower House had debated on the eight voting systems proposed by the ERC. The Commission recommended the combination of certain features of the FPTP System and the PR System as the most appropriate.

The Parliament has recently voted to adopt the PR System in the 224-seat Upper House, while retaining the current single–member-district plurality vote in the 400-member Lower House. On 16 January 2015, the Union Election Commission announced that the political parties are entitled to canvass for votes under Article 406 of the Constitution as well as to freedom of expression, peaceful gathering and procession under Article 354. The Chairman of the UEC determined a 60-day campaign period prior to the elections. It is one month less than the three-month timeframe allowed prior to the elections in 2010. However, there are still some concerns about certain restrictions on the political parties. For instance, the representatives of the political parties cannot campaign on behalf of their candidates without the approval of respective District Election Commission and campaigning parties have to provide the event schedule and time, venue and routes for the campaign rallies.

## The Issue of Support

Presently one of the most important issues of conjecture is that of support existing for each presidential candidate. Given that the amendment of the Articles in the Constitution could be realised before the elections and if

Daw Aung San Suu Kyi runs for the Presidency, it is expected that she would win the greatest support from the public, thus helping the NLD candidates contesting from different constituencies. As a consequence, the NLD might become a strong political force in the Parliament or at least a force to be reckoned with in every major political decision. In absence of her candidacy for the Presidency, both the incumbent President and the Speaker may hope to receive almost equal support from the public, although the President may expect to receive more public support because of his impressive achievements within a very short time span. However, it is more difficult to estimate the support of the President within his own party. Based on the news in various daily journals across the country, there have been rumours regarding solidarity within the party, and it is rumoured that the support for both the candidates is shifting and fluid. Another question is the support of the Armed Forces. If the Grand Parade that took place on the Independence Day of Myanmar is an indication, the President may receive more support from the Armed Forces. However, if the Commander-in-Chief confirms his candidacy for the Presidency he might, understandably, receive the support of the majority.

The candidacy of Daw Aung San Suu Kyi is linked to the amendment of Article 59(f) and consequently doubtful. However, she will certainly win a seat in the Lower House. The incumbent President also has not indicated any change in his publicly announced intention. Therefore his candidacy is also uncertain. Overall, the election process is progressing smoothly in spite of some unsolved issues. Given its experience of the 2010 elections, the UEC is capable of managing the whole process without any major hitch. The impact of the election results and its fairness is so significant for the democratisation of Myanmar and its continued economic development that the President and the Union Election Commission have become firmly committed to conducting the elections without any blemishes. As the most responsible organ under the Constitution, the UEC seems to be accommodating the legitimate concerns of all the political parties. This bodes well for the election. The Chairman of the UEC has stated that the UEC will invite international observers, although there will be a code of conduct established in accordance with the international norms. The presence of international observers will also be a contributing factor for holding free and fair election in Myanmar. No matter who among the current likely candidates is elected as President, the ongoing reform process will certainly continue and even be accelerated because a smooth and fair election may strengthen the trust of the international community in Myanmar. If the peace process cannot be concluded before the elections and if there are changes in the current representation on the Myanmarese side due to the change of government, the existing trust between the present administration and the ethnic armed groups has to be rebuilt to maintain the momentum. The President, therefore, stressed that it is imperative to merge the political development and the national reconciliation process. The 2015 election is the most important event for the Myanmarese people due to its impact on the future of the country as well as on their lives. The public interest in the election is very clear and obvious. As a result, the voters' turn-out may be greater than in the last elections and the party winning a clear victory will have a stronger mandate to move the country forward.

## Peace Process of Myanmar

The ethnic communities of Myanmar make up for 30 percent of its population. After the country's independence, there was a prolonged outbreak of violence in the country. In 1949, the Karen National Union went underground and armed conflicts between the government and ethnic armed groups broke out and lasted for more than six decades. Although the government had a round of ceasefires with the ethnic armed groups in the 1990s, these ceasefires did not lead to any political dialogue. The trust between the ethnic nationalists and the government decreased. When the government proposed in 2009 that some of these ethnic armed groups in a ceasefire agreement transform themselves into Border Guard Forces under the control of the Myanmar Armed Forces, the remaining trust was further undermined, and although some accepted the proposed transformation, others did not. In late 2011 and through 2012, the government of President U Thein Sein agreed to preliminary ceasefires with 10 of the 11 major ethnic armed groups. However, in June 2011, the Myanmar Army launched a major offensive against the Kachin Independence Organisation (KIO), the main Kachin Ethnic Armed Group, breaking a 17-year ceasefire and leading to displacement of tens of thousands of people and sporadic clashes between the Myanmar Army and the Kachin Independence Army—the armed wing of the KIO.

In May 2013, a preliminary truce was achieved between the Myanmar Government, the Army and the KIO. Since then, the leaders of major ethnic armed Groups, represented by the National Ceasefire Coordination Team (NCCT) and the Union Peace-making Working Committee (UPWC) have been negotiating for a nationwide ceasefire. The NCCT represents 16 armed groups, namely the Karen National Union (KNU), the Karen National Liberation Army (KNLA), the Democratic Karen Benevolent

Army (DKBA), the United Wa State Army (UWSA), the National Democratic Alliance Army (NDAA), the New Mon State Party (NMSP), the Arakan Liberation Party (ALP), the Shan State Progress Party (SSPP), the Shan State Army (SSA), the National Socialist Council of Nagaland (NSCN), the All Burma Students' Democratic Front (ABSDF), the Pa-o National Liberation Organization (PNLO), the Kachin Independence Army (KIA), the Ta'ang National Liberation Army (TNLA), the Karenni National Progressive Party (KNPP) and the Chin National Front.

There have already been six rounds of official talks between the Government's Union Peace-making Working Committee and the National Ceasefire Coordination Team. An agreement has been reached on further objectives such as a nationwide ceasefire agreement and the political dialogue. A nationwide ceasefire agreement is critical for the future of the country. There have been different views of the talks as regards their progress. According to U Aung Minn, Union Minister at the President's Office, who is also the leader of the Myanmarese side at the talks, the peace process is moving forward. Another different view is that the talks are deadlocked due to intransigent position of the government side. Some even argue that the realities on the ground for many people are much the same as before. They say that incidents of violence occur almost daily between the Myanmar Army and the KIO. They have also pointed out the continuing sporadic fighting even in areas where the ceasefires have been signed. During the recent visit of Myanmar's Vice President Dr Sai Mauk Kham to India in January 2015, India's President Pranab Mukherjee expressed his appreciation for the negotiation of a nationwide ceasefire with the armed ethnic groups. He also congratulated the Myanmar government for taking forward the peace and national reconciliation process in an inclusive manner to meet the aspirations of all the ethnic nationalities. Even though it is true that the peace process appears to be deadlocked, it has achieved a substantial progress. The achievement of a basic agreement, the continued engagement of both sides in the process, the demonstration of strong commitment of the political leadership to the achievement of peace with all ethnic armed groups, the existing ceasefire agreements with most of the ethnic armed groups, and much efforts that have been made to achieve a nation-wide ceasefire are very encouraging conditions to move the process forward.

The ethnic armed groups have been engaged in armed conflicts with the government for many years and consequently there has been a trust deficit between the two sides. With the fight still continuing, it is difficult to build trust quickly. The ethnic armed groups are suspicious that the army is not yet completely on board leading to differing positions on the government side. On the other hand, there have been disagreements among the ethnic armed groups which have further complicated the peace process. According to news reports, a major stumbling block is one of the demands of the Myanmar Army that the ethnic armed groups accept the 2008 Constitution. As they want a federal system, the ethnic armed groups want to amend the 2008 Constitution. The Myanmar peace process is extremely complicated because of the number of actors and interests at play but it is an inclusive process. A lot of key stakeholders are involved in the Myanmar peace process. They are the Myanmar Armed Forces and local militias; 16 ethnic armed groups including the Border Guard Forces and militias ethnic opposition alliances such as the United Nationalities Federal Council (UNFC) and the Working Group on Ethnic Coordination (WGEC), conflict-affected communities, civil society and national NGOs including exiled groups and border-based organisations, ethnic and other political parties, governments and donors, United Nations (UN) and other international organisations including the international NGOs, regional actors, business interests, refugees, diaspora communities and exiles. Key issues such as autonomy, management of natural resources and political representation remain unresolved and are still under discussion. A nationwide ceasefire is only a starting point and even after its achievement, there remains a long way to go before the success of the envisaged political dialogue. Nevertheless, the negotiations are continuing with faith and this is very encouraging indeed. So long as the negotiations go on with a firm commitment, there is always hope for a lasting peace in the country.

What is hindering the peace process, in addition to the key issues, is the continued conflict in the Kachin and the northern Shan State. As recently as on 9 February 2015, armed clashes between the Myanmar Armed Forces and the troops of the Myanmar National Democratic Alliance Army (MNDDA-Kokang Armed Group) a renegade group led by Phone Kya Shen, an ethnic leader broke out at the Nyankhwam village and the Tashwehtan village, southwest of Laukkai. In fact, the clashes broke out due to provocation by the group when it attacked the people's militia, the police forces in the villages and even the bases of the government armed forces. Some ethnic armed groups were also reported to have joined the renegade Kokang armed group in the fighting. This ethnic armed group was the very first group that had ceasefire agreement with the government in the 1990s. It will be very difficult for the peace process to move forward if these conflicts in Kachin and the northern Shan state are not ended immediately before they spiral out of control.

Myanmar has had over 60 years of conflict with the ethnic armed groups. In view of the present democratisation process and the international community poised to help the country, this is the perfect time to achieve a national reconciliation that will lead to peace, a stable democracy and foster economic development of the country. Though slow, the continuing negotiations show very positive signs. However, its success or failure will have serious implications. The Myanmarese history is not favourable in this regard. With persistent mistrust of the ethnic nationalities in the Myanmar government, the Ethnic Armed Groups will lose confidence in the government's sincerity if it fails to solve the nationality question as well as the conflicts between them and the military. The uniqueness of the Myanmarese peace process is that most of these groups already have ceasefire agreements with the government individually. These ceasefires are fragile at best and those armed groups are calling for an immediate stop to the government offensives as they think that most of these offensives have been initiated by the Myanmar Armed Forces. If these ceasefires break down as a consequence of continued conflicts or any new conflicts, it will threaten the overall political developments including the 2015 election. In their statement of 10 January 2013, the Shan State Progress Party (SSPP), the Shan State Party, the United Wa State Army (UWSA) and the National Democratic Alliance Army (NDAA) said they would revise their ceasefire agreements if the conflicts continue. These sentiments cannot be underestimated. The continued conflict will have an impact on the country's economic development for the following reasons. First of all, inevitably, the national defence budget will increase. Secondly, most of the natural resources of Myanmar exist in the ethnic regions and several mega projects are also in those areas (for instance, gas pipelines, industrial zones). The conflict may disrupt these foreign development projects. The Shwe Gas pipeline connecting China's Yunnan Province to Kyaukphyu in the Rakhine state of Myanmar is located in the northern Shan state where the Myanmar Armed Forces are clashing with the SSPP, SSA, KIA and TNLA. The disruption of present projects may keep away foreign investors away from Myanmar.

The armed conflicts in Myanmar has given rise to concerns in the neighbouring countries including China, India and Thailand where it has created a humanitarian crisis due to the outflow of refugees from the country. The fighting between the KIA and the Myanmar Armed Forces is said to have displaced over 100,000 civilians and thousands of them are in China. After the 2010 elections in Myanmar, there was an influx of nearly 18,000 civilians into Thailand due to clashes between the ethnic armed groups and the Myanmar army along the border. Similarly, taking advantage of the instability on the Myanmarese side, India's insurgents launched attacks in India. In the wake of the recent clash at Loukkai, the Chinese Foreign Ministry is reported to have indicated some concerns. The success in the peace process will certainly contribute to regional peace and security.

## Conclusion

The current peace process is designed to settle the question of nationalities once and for all and it is "a long journey", as recognised by the President at his meeting with the ethnic armed groups on 12 February 2015. Patience is essential to settle the ethnic problem deeply rooted in history and aggravated by the continued mistrust and hostilities between the central government and ethnic armed groups. The only choice left for all the stakeholders is to allow the current peace process to reach its conclusion and to have firm commitment to the success of the process. A very encouraging step in this regard has been the signing of "The Deed of Commitment for Peace and National Reconciliation" on the Union Day, under which all the signatories promised to "endeavour together" for the success of the peace process. The Deed was signed by the President, two Vice-Presidents, fourteen Union Ministers, five parliamentary representatives including two Speakers of the Parliament, the Chairman of the Union Election Commission, three representatives of the Armed Forces, ethnic armed groups, twenty-nine ethnic affairs ministers and fifty-five representatives from the political parties. There are some ethnic armed groups who have not signed the Deed yet. They will sign after discussions have been held and approved by their organisations. There is no doubt that the peace process efforts will continue until they achieve "a Nation-wide Ceasefire Agreement" following which "the Framework for Political Dialogue" will take place. This is a firm commitment of all the stakeholders and it is hoped that the peace process will be successful.

# 4

# Perceptions on India-Myanmar Relations

*Laldinkima Sailo*

In September 2011, the President of Myanmar, U Thein Sein, suspended the construction of a controversial $3.6 billion Chinese-led dam project amid public outcry, media attacks and campaign by civil society groups. While announcing the decision of the government, President Sein said his government had to act "according to the desire of the people".[1] In turn, China's reaction was that of shock and anger. An official of China Power Investment, the primary funder of the project, termed the decision as something that would incur "immeasurable" costs to both the countries and a Chinese Foreign Ministry spokesperson questioned the basis of the suspension of the project.[2] Questions on the relationship between the two Asian nations dominated discussions following the event.

Even as Myanmar embarked on a road to democratic reforms, with increasing space for participation by the media, civil society and public in influencing the government's decision, the incident underscored the role of public opinion in the government's decision, its interlinking relationship with the media and how this in turn can impact bilateral relations.

China has since embarked on a public relations exercise to placate the concerns of the affected community and to influence public opinion in its favour. In December 2013, China Power Investment released a corporate social responsibility report explaining the benefits of the dam for the local areas and its inhabitants.[3]

The continuation of democratic reforms and preparations to hold elections means that public opinion is likely to play an increasing role in the politics and policymaking in Myanmar. Just as the case of Myitsone dam shows that perceptions can impact bilateral relations, this is also true for India–Myanmar relations. This paper assesses the role of perception and provides a nuanced understanding of issues related to perception in the relationship.

As such, in the literature, much has been written about the role of public opinion and the media in policymaking—in particular, foreign policy. There are differing views on how these two impact policymakers. The issue is further compounded by questions of whether media influences the public and policymakers or is it in turn influenced by them.

## Public Opinion, Media and Foreign Policy

The two ends of the debate on the role of public opinion and its influence on foreign policymaking are represented by ideas that public opinion is volatile, emotional, lacking in coherence and structure, with little influence on foreign affairs, on the one hand,[4] and on the other end, that public opinion is stable, sensibly structured, consistent and influences foreign policymaking.[5]

The debate is juxtaposed by the argument that a freer media, represented by a growing fourth estate that has gained increased capability to gather information and disseminate it to a larger section of the population much more quickly than ever before, through the advancement of social media and 24-hour live news channels, has proliferated rapidly and this therefore informs the public.

Yet, the media's own relations with foreign policy is still debated. At the height of the debate, the *CNN effect* came to be understood as shorthand for the notion that mainstream news in general has an increased effect upon foreign policy formulation.[6] This notion was undergirded by the idea that ideological narratives play an important role in gaining public support for a particular line of action or in reinforcing of viewpoints, either of which in turn can influence the final decision. Robinson (2013)[7] argues that while recognising the power of ideological narratives, "it is also the case that governments have devoted increasing resources and time to attempt to shape and influence public perceptions in ways conducive to their preferred policies". The process has been variously termed as *perception management, strategic communication, public diplomacy* and recently, *global engagement* where the effort has focused on leveraging considerable resources at the disposal of governments in order to dominate the information environment.

The *CNN effect* is however disputed by scholars who argue that despite the revolution in communication technologies, politics still exerts an influence on the media than vice versa[8] and that media is often susceptible to manipulation by politicians at the helm of policymaking and practitioners of foreign policymaking who can withhold information. Yet, even this group would argue that there are cases where the media can indeed influence foreign policy, such as in following situations:[9]

1. Where there is a lack of consensus among the elite over the strategic issues or a specific policy option;
2. When the policy of the government or of international units is inconsistent and wavering;
3. In cases of loose political control over the situation;
4. When the foreign policy process is in its final stages;
5. In cases of bad communication to the public about the decisions taken;
6. When there is a high level of free access to information.

The nuances in the debate around public policy, media and foreign policy is however made clear in the autobiography of Hillary Clinton, *Hard Choices* (2014), where she argues and justifies the prioritising of public diplomacy initiatives as an important aspect of her role as the chief diplomat of the United States, to ensure continued public support at home and abroad—both of which are seen as important in the success of numerous foreign policy initiatives of the country.

## Public Diplomacy and India

The idea of managing perceptions and outreach to the media and the public has also recently become an important part of India's foreign policy, though it still has a long way to go. When Dr S. Jaishankar took over as the Foreign Secretary in 2015, he outlined the need for engaging the media and inter alia the public and said, "I know that the media is an important part of our foreign policy projection."[10]

India's Ministry of External Affairs established a Public Diplomacy division in 2006. Their aim was to "educate and influence global and domestic opinion on key policy issues and project a better image of the country commensurate with its rising international standing."[11] The promotion of India's image abroad is also aided by the Indian Council for Cultural Relations (ICCR), which remains the pre-eminent instrument of cultural diplomacy, while the Ministry of Information and Broadcasting debate lends support to the public diplomacy initiative with the Ministry's strategic use of the media, which is "responsible for international cooperation in the field of mass media, films and broadcasting and interaction with its foreign counterparts on behalf of the government of India".[12]

The Indian Brand Equity Foundation in collaboration with the Ministry of Commerce and Industry, Government of India, and the Confederation of Indian Industry also has embarked on public relations and branding initiatives where the "primary objective is to build positive economic perceptions of India globally. It aimed to effectively present the Indian business perspective and leverage business partnerships in a globalising market-place." There is an increased recognition that there is a need to build India's image at home as well as abroad to attract investments as and to bolster the image of the Indian public sector and the private-sector companies abroad.

Despite all these efforts, India is not yet seen leveraging the enormous soft power and goodwill at its disposal to its full potential. The following chapter analyses the way perceptions plays a role in India—Myanmar relationship that is both broad-based and multifaceted.

## India–Myanmar Relations: An Overview

India and Myanmar share a land border of 1643 km and a maritime boundary in the Bay of Bengal. The two countries have shared historical, cultural and religious ties that date back as far as the third century BC. A large population of Indians (according to some estimates, 2–3 million) live in Myanmar and trace their migration from India during the colonial period.

Since both the countries gained independence from British rule over 60 years ago, the relationship has seen several ups and downs. India's support to the democratic movement in Myanmar in the late 1980s is seen as yielding space to China which dominated Myanmar's relation with its neighbours for the last two decades. Despite the overtures made by India in the early 1990s towards the junta that had ruled Myanmar since 1988, it faced a dilemma and risked alienating its support for democracy and activists on one hand and giving China a free hand in expanding its influence in the region on the other.

Several insurgent groups operating in Northeast India were also based out of Myanmar and despite efforts, relations between the two countries were bracketed in security issues, democracy and historical experiences.

However, Myanmar's political reforms and re-entry into the

international stage has allowed India to develop a much more broad-based relationship. One of the explanations for the changes taking place in Myanmar is its attempt to free itself from the tight embrace of China and to allow a wider range of engagements with its neighbours and the rest of the world. In creating this space, there is an expectation that India, along with other countries in the Southeast Asia region and Japan, will fill the gap and intensify their engagement.

At the moment, India's absence in Myanmar is conspicuous and any mention of India tends to get hyphenated into a comparison with China where the latter is seen as a country that is dynamic and the former as chaotic.[13] Despite an increasing resentment against Chinese presence, particularly in the economic realm in Myanmar, there is a sense of awe and aspiration with which the growth of China is portrayed. Whereas Chinese goods and brands dot marketplaces, Indian brands are yet to make their presence felt.

India's current commitments, including $25 million over five years in the Naga self-administered areas of Myanmar and $750 million soft line of credit as well as an Agriculture/Rice Bio Park which adds up to approximately $1.25 billion of assistance,[14] are enormously significant even in comparative terms, but are largely unreported.

Given that a large number of Myanmarese who found refuge in India during the reign of the junta have returned to the country, there is also an expectation among this group that India would step up its presence in Myanmar.

Despite the earlier disappointment of being overlooked as India looked east, the increasing importance that India places on Myanmar—as a way of bringing new economic dynamism and development to its landlocked Northeast—as part of its evolving Look East Policy is being welcomed in the country.

Since Mr Thein Sein took over as President of Myanmar in 2011, several high-level visits have taken place and India has committed to a number of assistance and cooperation projects. These commitments encompass a range of projects which Myanmar expects will enable it to move towards economic development and closer relationship with India. However, there are concerns about India's capacity and political will to see through the (timely) delivery of these promises.

## Indian Projects in Myanmar

The Government of India is actively involved in a number of projects in

Myanmar, both in the infrastructural and non-infrastructural areas. These include upgradation of the 160km long Tamu-Kalewa-Kalemyo road; construction of the Rih-Tiddim Road in Myanmar that connects with Mizoram and the Kaladan Multi-Modal Transport Project. ONGC Videsh Ltd. (OVL), GAIL and ESSAR have invested in the energy sector in Myanmar. M/s RITES is involved in the development of the rail transportation system, and a truck assembly plant was set up by TATA Motors in Myanmar in 2010. There are also industrial training centres, an English language school, an entrepreneurship development centre and an IT training centre developed with India's assistance that are operational.[15]

Other projects include renovation of the Ananda Temple in Bagan, upgradation of the Yangon Children's Hospital and the Sittwe General Hospital, building of disaster-proof rice silos and building of schools in the Tarlay township.[16]

In 2008, India's NHPC had signed an agreement for the development of the Tamanthi (1200 MW) and Shwezaye (880 MW) Hydro-Electric Power project in the Chindwin River valley. These projects were however dropped in 2013 on grounds that the potential (adverse) social and environmental impact did not justify the economic benefits of the project.[17] Several media reports and civil society groups had been highlighting the adverse impact of the Tamanthi project.[18] Further, this comes close on the heels of the cancellation of the Myitsone dam project, which was being built by the state-owned Chinese Power Investment Corporation (CPI) following protests by local communities and environmental groups.

The political change and move towards democracy in Myanmar has provided space to the media and non-governmental organisations which were hitherto clamped down. Through the media and NGOs, communities are much more vocal in raising their concerns regarding huge infrastructure and development projects than they had been earlier. And, today, the political leadership across the board and in particular the current military-backed government are more accommodating of the views of a diverse section of society, including the views of the affected communities.

Some sections of the media and civil society groups have also raised questions about the "implementation of the Kaladan Project regarding its policies on human rights, indigenous rights, community consultation, environmental impact assessment, local hiring and labour conditions".[19] There is also palpable resentment over the fact that an environmental impact assessment had not been carried out either by the Indian company or the Myanmarese government.

As such, the conditions with which the Chinese companies have participated in the infrastructure and natural resources sector—such as in the above-mentioned Myitsone Dam case—including appropriating the benefit of the resources, non-hiring of locals, displacement, etc, have caused great resentment against the Chinese businesses in the country.

## Trade and Business

Trade between India and Myanmar has seen a steady growth, albeit with slight decline from time to time, since the signing of the India and Myanmar Trade Agreement in 1970. Bilateral trade stood at US$ 1.92 billion in 2012–13,[20] with a target of US$ 3 billion by 2015. The agriculture sector dominates the bilateral trade, Myanmar is the second largest supplier of beans and pulses to India, next only to Canada, accounting for one-third of India's total requirement of imported pulses. India imported pulses and beans worth $ 1090 million from Myanmar. Myanmar also contributes nearly one-fifth of India's import of timber. Timber and wood products have accounted for more than 37 percent of Myanmar's exports to India ($ 400 million). Other items of trade include pharmaceutical products, steel and iron products, electrical machinery, mineral oil, rubber and articles, plastics, etc.[21]

Despite these figures, there is a feeling on both sides in India and Myanmar that the current levels are far below the potential. Moreover, the figures pale in comparison to those of Myanmar's other neighbours. Trade between Myanmar and Thailand was worth $5.57 billion[22] during the fiscal year that ended in March 2014, with a goal of increasing that to $6.1 billion by 2015.[23] Myanmar has a huge trade surplus with Thailand because oil and gas account for a large share of its $4.2 billion in exports, while imports from Thailand to Myanmar have been worth $1.36 billion. The main products imported to Myanmar from Thailand are food, electronic goods, construction materials and home appliances.

Trade between China and Myanmar in the 2013–14 fiscal year was valued at more than $7 billion, which included $4 billion in imports from China. Trade with Bangladesh however remains low at $100 million.[24]

Along with India, three of these countries that also share a border with Myanmar maintain border trade with it. The total border trade turnover for Myanmar with all its neighbours was $4.46 billion during the 2013–14 fiscal year.[25] There are huge challenges in quantifying border trade figures with all of the neighbours but there are strong evidences to show that China and Thailand account for a significant part of Myanmar's border trade. Officials at the Union of Myanmar Federation of Chambers of Commerce and Industry (UMFCCI) ruefully told a delegation from the Institute of South Asian Studies (ISAS) that border trade with India is even lower than the trade with Bangladesh.

The UMFCCI officials lamented that despite a similar production base, consumer tastes and complementary small and medium enterprises between Myanmar and India, the Northeast in particular, border trade between these two have remained low. Several Memorandums of Understanding (MoU) have been signed between the industry associations in India and Myanmar including those between the UMFCCI and the Confederation of Indian Industry (CII) and between the Myanmar–India Business Club and the Federation of Industries and Commerce of North-Eastern Region (FINER). Yet, there is a sense that these have not led to anything substantial and there has been lack of encouragement from either the government of Myanmar or of India.

Besides the promotion of trade per se, there are however other areas where businesses in Myanmar can eye India as a potential partner.. These include the provision of training and skills, such as in international taxation, negotiation and in understanding of regulatory frameworks that would enable Myanmarese companies to internationalise. The ISAS delegation was told that a past training session conducted by India's Institute of Foreign Trade (IIFT) had been very useful for businesses in Myanmar.

## Media Perceptions

One of the issues that seem to hinder the effective moving forward of border trade from the Myanmarese side is one encompassing the outstanding issues involving the borders. There is a section of Myanmarese officials and scholars who view border issues as a 'dispute', where Indian constructions have been termed as 'incursions'[26] while India views this differently. Answering a question posed by an MP from Manipur, Smt Preneet Kaur, the then Minister of State (MoS) for External Affairs told, the Lok Sabha in December 2013 that "there is no boundary dispute between India and Myanmar. There are, however, nine unresolved Boundary Pillars (BP) along the India-Myanmar Border in Manipur sector."[27]

Some in Myanmar feel that other than on the above-mentioned issue, there are wide-ranging differences in perceptions that largely emanate from a lack of knowledge about each other. Mainstream media on both sides writes very little about the other and an editor of a Myanmar daily is of the view that the people in Myanmar know much more about China and US than India.[28]

The lack of understanding and the portrayal of each other also creates and exacerbates the perceptions such as those mentioned earlier regarding India's political will and seriousness. Take for instance, the operationalisation of the flight from Mandalay to Imphal, on which the *Myanmar Times* reported, "The launch of a planned air route between Mandalay and Imphal in northern India has been delayed while logistical details are finalised with Indian authorities" where "the delays are thought to be related to immigration rules for incoming passengers"[29] meaning a delay from the Indian side. On the other hand, the view from the Indian side usually puts reasons for the delay on the Myanmarese side.

## Regional Engagements

India shares a platform with Myanmar at several regional forums. Significantly, these include the Bay of Bengal Initiative for Multi-Sectoral Technical and Economic Cooperation (BIMSTEC), the Mekong Ganga Cooperation (MGC), the East Asia Summit and the South Asian Association for Regional Cooperation (2008) where Myanmar was given the status of observer in 2008.

India plays a significant role in these groupings and as the biggest partner in BIMSTEC, MGC and SAARC, there is an expectation that India will take the lead in working towards the establishment of physical connectivity and the creation of an integrated tourism circuit, be it in the provision of funds or in the churning out of technical details where it has a larger resource pool than other member countries.

## Managing Perceptions

There is an opportunity for India to leverage on the goodwill that it has generated overseas. India is also seen as a global power in terms of its soft power which can be strategically employed in the process of developing an image that is vibrant, friendly and also efficient.

The management of perception which can go a long way for not only the government but also for the Indian companies doing business abroad will need a concerted effort to rectify. While the government can expand its public diplomacy initiatives to engage media in its host countries, there is also a need to address some of the root causes of the perception issues. This includes the timely delivery of promises made and the completion of such projects.

An enhanced perception in turn makes it easier for the government of partner nations, such as Myanmar, to further their own engagement with India. The apprehension of the rise of China and the high expectation generated by the renewed economic dynamism as well as its entrepreneurial spirit provides a low hanging fruit of opportunity, which India must seize.

## NOTES

1. Aung Hla Tun, "Myanmar Shelves $3.6 Billion Mega Dam, Officials Say", *Reuters*, 30 September 2011, http://www.reuters.com/article/2011/09/30/us-myanmar-dam-idUSTRE78T10H20110930
2. Jonathan Watts, "China Angry over Burma's Decision to Suspend Work on £2.3Bn Dam", *The Guardian*, 4 October 2011, http://www.theguardian.com/environment/2011/oct/04/china-angry-burma-suspend-dam.
3. Yun Sun, "China, Myanmar Face Myitsone Dam Truths", *The Asia Times*, 19 February 2014, http://www.atimes.com/atimes/Southeast_Asia/SEA-01-190214.html
4. See Holsti, Ole R. (1996), *Public Opinion and American Foreign Policy*, Ann Arbor: University of Michigan Press; also, Foyle, Douglas (1999), *Counting the Public In: Presidents, Public Opinion, and Foreign Policy*, New York: Columbia University Press.
5. Katz, Andrew Z. (1997), "Public Opinion and Foreign Policy: The Nixon Administration and the Pursuit of Peace with Honor in Vietnam", *Presidential Studies Quarterly*, 27.3.
6. Robinson, Piers (2013), "Media as a Driving Force in International Relations: The CNN Effect and Related Debates", *E-International Relations*.
7. Ibid.
8. Yordanova, Tsvetelina (2012), "Media-International Relations Interaction Model", Research Report 26, Institute for Security and International Studies (ISIS), Sofia.
9. Ibid.
10. "S. Jaishankar, Former Envoy to US, Takes Charge as the New Foreign Secretary", *NDTV*, 29 January 2015. http://www.ndtv.com/video/player/news/s-jaishankar-former-envoy-to-us-takes-charge-as-the-new-foreign-secretary/354577.
11. Ritambhara (2013), "On Indian Diplomacy", *E-International Relations Publishing*.
12. Ministry of Information and Broadcasting, Government of India. http://mib.nic.in/information/audiovideo/frames.html.
13. Based on the author's interviews with scholars, former diplomats and mediapersons.
14. Comments by Mr Gautam Mukhopadhyay, Ambassador of India to Myanmar at the 'Shillong Dialogue', organised by the Asian Confluence and the Indian Council of World Affairs, Dec 5-6, 2014, Shillong.
15. 'India-Myanmar Relations', Ministry of External Affairs, India. http://www.mea.gov.in/Portal/ForeignRelation/India-Myanmar_Relations.pdf.

16. "Development Cooperation Projects Undertaken by the Government of India", Embassy of India, Yangon, Myanmar. http://www.indiaembassyyangon.net/index.php?option=com_content&view=category&layout=blog&id=23&Itemid=124&lang=en.
17. Utpal Bhaskar, "Myanmar Scraps Two Hydroelectric Projects Planned with India", *Livemint*, 06 June 2013. http://www.livemint.com/Politics/tDFDnAVpqiWv8osH8RePhL/Myanmar-scraps-two-hydroelectric-projects-planned-with-India.html.
18. "Burma Rivers Network Welcomes India's Cancellation of Tamanthi Dam, Urges China and Thailand to Take Similar Environmental Responsibility", Statement by the Burma Rivers Network. http://burmariversnetwork.org/index.php/actions/press-releases/907-burma-rivers-network-welcomes-indias-cancellation-of-tamanthi-dam-urges-china-and-thailand-to-take-similar-environmental-responsibility.
19. Bill O' Toole, "India Stands by Controversial Kaladan Transport Project", *Myanmar Times*, 30 June 2014. http://www.mmtimes.com/index.php/national-news/10862-india-stands-by-controversial-kaladan-transport-project.html.
20. "Myanmar", India-Myanmar Business Promotion Council, The Associated Chambers of Commerce and Industry of India. www.assocham.org/international/india-bilateral-trade/52.-mayanmar.docx.
21. "Bilateral and Economic Relations" Embassy of India, Yangon, Myanmar. http://www.indiaembassyyangon.net/index.php?option=com_content&view=category&layout= blog&id=21&Itemid=122&lang=en.
22. Grace Kyaw, "Trade on the Rise along Myanmar's Busy Borders", *Bangkok Post*, 19 May 2014. http://www.bangkokpost.com/business/news/410573/trade-on-the-rise-along-myanmar-busy-borders.
23. Petchanet Pratruangkrai, "Thailand, Myanmar Aim to Triple Trade by 2015", *The Nation*, 3 November 2012. http://www.nationmultimedia.com/business/Thailand-Myanmar-aim-to-triple-trade-by-2015-30193589.html.
24. "Bangladesh-Myanmar to Boost Bilateral Trade to $500m", *Dhaka Tribune*, 19 January 2014. http://www.dhakatribune.com/commerce/2014/jan/19/bangladesh-myanmar-boost-bilateral-trade-500m.
25. Grace Kyaw, "Trade on the Rise along Myanmar's Busy Borders", *Bangkok Post*, 19 May 2014. http://www.bangkokpost.com/business/news/410573/trade-on-the-rise-along-myanmar-busy-borders. Accessed 8 July 2014.
26. "MP Warns Border Dispute with India could Lead to 'Serious Unrest'", *Mizzima News*, 30 December 2013. http://www.mizzima.com/mizzima-news/regional/item/10774-mp-warns-border-dispute-with-india-could-lead-to-serious-unrest.
27. "Q No 2165 Indo-Myanmar Border Dispute", Lok Sabha Unstarred Question, answered on 18 December 2013, Ministry of External Affairs, India.http://www.mea.gov.in/lok-sabha.htm?dtl/22666/Q+NO2165+INDOMYANMAR+BORDER+DISPUTE.
28. Editor, *Mizzima News* at an ISAS workshop held in Yangon, March 2014.
29. Zaw Win Than and Bill O' Toole, "Mandalay, Imphal Flight Launch Delayed", *Myanmar Times*, 30 June 2014. http://www.mmtimes.com/index.php/national-news/10863-mandalay-imphal-flight-launch-delayed.html.

# 5

# Re-Imagining Neighbourhood Ties: Looking Beyond Bilateralism

*K. Yhome*

Bangladesh, India and Myanmar share long land and maritime boundaries with rich historical and cultural ties and form the key littorals of the Bay of Bengal. Bilateral relations among the three neighbours have seen ups and downs, but in recent years ties with each other have witnessed greater cordiality and understanding. Located in the north-eastern part of the Indian Ocean, the Bay of Bengal is the most important feature that defines the region's geography and binds the three countries in the maritime domain. The three countries also have the geographical advantage of being linked by land as Bangladesh presents itself as a bridge between India and Myanmar, thereby linking South and Southeast in continental Asia.

These characteristics make the three countries a compact geographical space. In fact, it was this geographical proximity that made possible easy movement of people across the Bay for several centuries creating not only deep cultural and historical ties but also a common ecological space. Rulers in different periods of time had built or aspired to build a common political empire for the entire region which was achieved during the British Raj in India in the nineteenth century. Criss-crossing historical, cultural, economic and ecological linkages have shaped the evolution of their relationships and the region as a whole. This rhetoric has so far failed to be translated into reality. The present scenario provides an opportunity to redefine the relationships of the three neighbours as all the countries are increasingly moving away from their inward-looking approach to re-engage and reset their ties with their neighbours and the international community.

This paper argues that there is a strong basis for trilateralism among the three countries. There are both internal and external factors that are opening up huge opportunities for the three countries to work together in the interest of each nation and the wider Bay of Bengal region. The first section examines recent developments in the three nations with an aim to highlight how the internal changes could be taken advantage of to strengthen relations. The second section looks at initiatives beyond bilateralism in the Bay of Bengal region and explores the possibilities of trilateralism among the three countries and explores the potential areas for cooperation.

## Leveraging Changes

There have been significant political and economic developments in all the three countries and in the entire Bay of Bengal region in recent years that could be leveraged to strengthen and expand ties among them. If India and Myanmar are promising new aspirations as a result of recent political and economic changes, Bangladesh is slowly consolidating what it has achieved in the recent past. Even as the paths to deepening democracy and economic development in all the three countries seem unlikely to derail, there are daunting challenges in meeting the stated goals. But, the current leaderships in all the three countries have demonstrated that they are committed to change.

## Myanmar: Opening up

One of the most significant developments in the Bay of Bengal region in the recent past has been Myanmar's re-engagement with the international community after several decades of isolation. The opening up of the Southeast Asian nation in 2011 has triggered a renewed geopolitical interest among the global players to re-engage a region that has often been seen as a strategic backwater. With a long coastline straddling the Bay of Bengal just north of the strategic Sea Lines of Communications in the Indian Ocean and close to the Malacca Straits, Myanmar is also the largest country in continental Southeast Asia with rich natural resources including gold, precious stones, oil and gas. Its location at the cross-roads of South, Southeast and East Asia makes the country a geo-strategically important area for all the major players.

The new "civilian" government under President Thein Sein that took power in 2011 has initiated unprecedented political, legal and socio-economic reforms. The transition to democracy in Myanmar has had huge implications not only inside the country but also in its foreign policy orientations. The Western countries including the US, European Union (EU) and Japan are back in the country after several years of imposing sanctions and isolating Myanmar. The country is today engaging both its neighbours and other global players with the aim to revive its economy and also to rebalance its foreign relations. The reforms have brought about impressive economic performance in the recent years with GDP growth averaging at six percent since 2011 and most estimates suggest that the country's growth will accelerate to over eight percent in the next couple of years.

The opening up of the country has also positively impacted its relations with India. For India, Myanmar's reforms have given it an opportunity to scale up its cooperation with the country in every sector from infrastructure to health and education. One of the fallouts of the transition of Myanmar that has negatively impacted its relations with Bangladesh has been the issue of Rohingyas – a Muslim minority community that Myanmar alleges are from Bangladesh.[1] Fresh violence targeting the Rohingyas in Myanmar's Rakhine State has pushed hundreds of refugees into bordering Bangladesh.[2] Even as the issue remains a thorny issue, the governments of both the countries have not made the issue cast its shadow over their overall bilateral relationship.[3]

## Bangladesh: Reaching Out

Growing at more than six percent for much of the past one decade, Bangladesh's is one of the fastest growing nations in South Asia. Despite frequent political turmoil with the tendency to hit the streets on every issue, crippling economic life, a steady rise in economic growth has further pushed the leadership to reach out to the international community for deepening economic ties. The country is also looking at deepening ties with its neighbourhood as further trans-border connectivity with improved infrastructure facilities will have a positive impact on the country's expanding trade and capability to attract investment.

In the recent past, India–Bangladesh relations have strengthened and deepened under Prime Minister Sheikh Hasina. Major positive developments have been in the settlement of land and maritime boundary disputes (discussed below) and in Bangladesh emerging as the largest trading partner of India in South Asia. As discussed above, the Rohingya issue remains a difficult issue between Bangladesh and Myanmar. However, both the countries are looking forward to cooperate in areas of mutual benefits. This thrust was reiterated by the leaders of the two countries during the visit of Prime Minister Sheikh Hasina to Myanmar in March 2014 on the eve of the summit meeting of the Bay of Bengal Initiative for Multi-Sectoral Technical and Economic Cooperation (BIMSTEC). The two countries also agreed to resolve the refugee issue "amicably" and stressed on economic development to strengthen bilateral relationship.

In the recent past, the two countries have been exploring ways to expand their economic ties. For instance, Bangladesh has proposed cross-border electricity trade in exchange of gas from Myanmar. According to a Bangladeshi proposal, the gas from Myanmar's Chin State would be transported through a pipeline to a power plant in Chittagong and the power generated would then be exported again to Myanmar.[4] In fact, as early as 2010, the two countries had initiated a cross-border electricity trade.[5] Recently, there has been a new move to build a road to link their border towns with the aim to boost border trade.[6]

## India: "Neighbourhood First" Policy

Prime Minister Narendra Modi's "neighbourhood first" policy has given a renewed push to reset India's ties with its immediate neighbours and this provides an opportune time to explore greater cooperation and coordination between the three countries. For some time now, there is a strong recognition that India's prosperity lies in the prosperity of the entire region and that India cannot prosper alone but needs to take the region along. With this thinking New Delhi is willing to share its economic prosperity with the whole region. This vision was again articulated by Prime Minister Modi at the 18th SAARC Summit in November 2014 in Kathmandu when he said that his vision for the "region rests on five pillars – trade, investment, assistance, cooperation in every area, contacts between our people – and, all through seamless connectivity" based on the belief that the region's destiny is "inter-linked".[7]

Since coming to power in May 2014, Prime Minister Modi has committed to reset India's relation with the immediate neighbours and in order to achieve that Modi has proposed various measures to integrate the region. At the SAARC summit, Modi proposed a "SAARC business traveller card"; creation of a "special purpose facility" for infrastructure projects; and to create cross-border industrial corridors and common electricity grids while emphasising for greater air, road and rail connectivity among the countries of the region.[8] If one looks at these proposals, in the backdrop of what Modi has been doing in the domestic realm with his emphasis on connectivity infrastructure aimed at connecting the border states and extending it to the neighbouring countries as well as making more space for these states to play a role in regional diplomacy, then all these suggest that the current government is charting out a new road map to cement India's relationship with its immediate neighbours.

## Settlement of the Boundary Disputes

One of the most important developments in India–Bangladesh relationship has been the settlement of the long-standing issue of land boundary dispute. The ratification of the Land Boundary Agreement (LAB) of 1974 by the Indian Parliament has enabled the two countries to exchange land (or enclaves) in each other's territory, thus resolving the problem of adversely possessed land. The significance of the agreement is enormous as it demonstrates that both the countries are willing to resolve sensitive issues amicably and this has raised new hopes in widening the bilateral relationship.[9]

Another significant development that presents an opportunity for the three countries to leverage for building mutual trust and for entering into joint ventures is the settlement of the vexed issue of maritime boundary disputes. For several years, the maritime dispute has been a bone of contention in the bilateral relationships between the disputing countries, namely between India and Bangladesh as well as between Myanmar and Bangladesh. In March 2012, the International Tribunal on the Law of the Sea announced its verdict on the dispute between Bangladesh and Myanmar.[10] Two years later, in July 2014, The Hague-based Permanent Court of Attribution gave its verdict on the maritime dispute between India and Bangladesh ending the long dispute between the two countries.[11] The settlement of maritime disputes and the acceptance of the verdict by all the countries show another important point that international norms and rules are being upheld and respected. Moreover, the settlement of maritime disputes has opened up new opportunities for the three countries to exploit natural resources, particularly oil and gas. Joint development in these areas can be explored by the three countries.

## Growing Infrastructure Development

A development that is increasingly changing the importance of the Bay of Bengal and which in turn is driving the new geopolitics of the region is the massive infrastructural projects that are coming up in the littoral nations. For several decades, the lack of infrastructure has been a major reason the Bay of Bengal region has lagged behind its neighbouring

Southeast Asian tiger economies. The recent infrastructure developments are opening up the Bay to connect the countries with the wider region's production and supply chain. This has also triggered competition among the major players in the development of the much-needed infrastructure facilities such as ports, roads, railways, and waterways, hydropower, oil and gas exploration, etc. For instance, China has been involved in infrastructure development of projects like ports, pipelines, dams in Myanmar and Sri Lanka while India has been building ports, roads and waterways in Myanmar and Sri Lanka. The opening up of Myanmar has attracted more players in the sector. Japan's is coming in a big way in developing the region's infrastructure with the announcement of the Bay of Bengal Industrial Growth Belt or the "B-Big" initiative. The growing connectivity infrastructure facilities in and around the Bay of Bengal are further connecting the three countries.

At a time when the geopolitics of the Bay is undergoing rapid changes, there is an urgent need for the key littorals to work more closely in a cooperative framework to take full advantage of the emerging opportunities and address the challenges to ensure that these changes do not adversely affect their interests. There is a need to work together to shape the evolving geopolitics of the region as overlapping geopolitical interests of the major powers increasingly redefine the future of the Bay of Bengal. In fact, some observers situate the Bay of Bengal within the evolving geopolitical dynamics of the Indo-Pacific region and argue that the Bay is increasingly emerging at the centre of these changes.[12] Given these developments, there are huge opportunities as well as challenges for the three countries to cooperate and coordinate their policies.

## Rise in NTS

The issue of non-traditional security threats (NTS) in the region presents itself in both the continental and the maritime domains. In fact, there is a close link between the two when it comes to NTS. Although maritime piracy in the Bay of Bengal has not emerged as a major challenge as compared to other parts of the world, reports of accidents of piracy, smuggling of arms and ammunitions and human trafficking have been on the rise in the area. A new dimension that has added to these security challenges is maritime terrorism, particularly in the context of the extremist elements in the littoral countries.

According to the Regional Cooperation Agreement on Combating Piracy and Armed Robbery against Ships in Asia (ReCAAP) Information Sharing Centre (ISC), the number of piracy incidents reported in 2014 in

South Asia has increased from the previous year owning to an increase of such incidents in Bangladesh.[13] Although most of the incidents are petty thefts involving robbing fishermen or abducting them for ransom, there have been incidents of killing fishermen such as the killing of over a dozen Bangladeshi fishermen by pirates in March 2013.[14] Reports of pirate attacks have continued in the recent times. In February 2015, there were reports of pirate attacks on Bangladeshi fishermen.[15] Several analysts have suggested that piracy is emerging as a real threat in the Bay of Bengal.[16]

Recognising the need to step up vigilance and cooperation, a few initiatives have been taken towards addressing these issues. India has been conducting joint military exercises and joint patrols with several countries in the Bay of Bengal to combat maritime terrorism, piracy as well as focus on natural disaster relief operations. Navy-to-Navy exchanges and dialogues among the three countries have increased over the years with the first India–Myanmar joint naval exercise conducted in 2013 and the Myanmar Navy participating in the biennial MILAN joint exercise hosted by the Indian Navy in the Andaman and Nicobar Islands.[17] The other area that has emerged as an area for cooperation is in the HADR. The Bay of Bengal has been known for fierce tropical cyclones with devastating consequences. In fact, the Indian Navy has been an active player in disaster relief operations in the region.

## Trilateralism: An Alternative Approach[18]

Several instruments and mechanisms exist in various sectors between the three countries, at the bilateral as well as multilateral levels, that aim to strengthen ties for mutual benefits. Much has been achieved through such cooperation and coordination, though there is room to make the arrangements more effective to tap the full potential of these mechanisms. The present scenario as presented above provides an opportunity to imagine innovative ways to expand and deepen neighbourhood ties with the aim to inject a new dynamism in the existing level of cooperation. Increasingly, there has been a growing support to the idea that a regional approach is required to address the emerging issues and challenges confronting the region.

For instance, the regional dimension of environmental issues calls for a regional approach to the problem. Even in the security sphere, there is an increasing call for regional cooperation and collaboration in tackling NTS issues. The rationale behind this call is that issues such as climate change or NTS know no national boundaries. In fact, most of the emerging challenges transcend national boundaries. In the context of exploring possibilities for cooperation among Bangladesh, India and Myanmar, there are a few concepts that may be explored to understand how trilateral cooperation can be operationalised. The first is the concept of "trilateralism" that became popular in international politics in the 1970s when North America, Western Europe and Japan came together to form a non-governmental grouping called the Trilateral Commission that was founded in 1973 to construct a common approach and coordinate policies on global political and economic issues.[19]

The second concept is that of "growth triangles" that has gained much currency in the Southeast Asian context in the recent past. Growth triangles are transnational economic zones that aim to take advantage of geographical proximity to exploit comparative advantage and synergies in a compact geographical space.[20] After the success in the first ASEAN growth triangle called the Singapore-Johor-Riau Growth Triangle (SIJORI) or the Southern IMS-GT (Indonesia-Malaysia-Singapore) in the late 1980s, other growth triangles have mushroomed in the region including the Northern IMT-GT (Indonesia-Malaysia-Thailand); the Eastern BIMP-EAGE (Brunei-Indonesia-Malaysia-Philippines) and also the Greater Mekong Sub-region involving Cambodia, Laos, Myanmar, Thailand, Vietnam and the Yunnan Province of China.

Closer home, the third concept is the "maritime security trilateralism"[21] involving India, Sri Lanka and the Maldives.[22] The trilateral maritime security arrangement began in October 2011 among the three neighbours with the aim to share capacities and information to deal with the growing maritime security threats in the form of piracy, terrorism, gunrunning and also to pursue a sustainable development of the maritime environment.[23] These trilateral initiatives have come about with a vision and as a response to a need.

The above discussion suggests that trilateralism as a concept can exist for various purposes and can involve three or more countries. The first two concepts are economic in origin, though the concept of trilateralism has a strategic dimension to maintain dominance over the global economy by the most powerful economic players. Trilateral cooperation is not, however, confined to economic cooperation. In fact, trilateral maritime security cooperation involving India, Sri Lanka and Maldives suggests that such a mechanism could play a vital role in enhancing mutual cooperation in the field of security. There is no reason why such an initiative cannot be explored among Bangladesh, India and Myanmar.

In fact, it may be pointed out that there have been attempts to look beyond bilateralism in the Bay of Bengal region in the past. The littoral countries have attempted at building several sub-regional groupings such as the BIMSTEC, the Ganga–Mekong Cooperation and the South Asia Growth Quadrangle with the aim of fostering regional integration. Also, there are transnational initiatives such as the Bangladesh-China-India and Myanmar Economic corridor, the India-Myanmar-Thailand Trilateral Highway, or the India-Myanmar Kaladan Multi-model Transit and Transport project that aims at strengthening regional connectivity. All these initiatives could be leveraged for building cooperation at the trilateral level.

Today, there are visions for a trilateral initiative in the region. One such vision was proposed by Prime Minister Modi in his speech at the SAARC summit in Kathmandu. On the other hand, the need for having such an initiative has long been felt in the region. With both the vision and the need in place, the time has come to act on them. To begin with, a few areas where the three countries could work together is in economic development, tourism, environmental issues, and security. These are spheres that will determine where the Bay of Bengal will stand compared to its neighbouring sub-regions in the years to come and these are also areas where the potential for cooperation among the littorals are most urgent. Early attempts to work towards this direction for cooperation will be an added advantage for the entire region.

India, Bangladesh and Myanmar are well placed to step up their cooperation in all these areas given the geographical contiguity and the level of development on all sides of their borders. Developing basic infrastructure is a prerequisite to increase economic activities in the border areas including border trade. For instance, Myanmar President Thein Sein has invited Bangladesh to be a partner in the India-Myanmar-Thailand Trilateral Highway initiative. Similarly, Bangladesh could be a partner in the India–Myanmar Kaladan project. The three countries could also work towards facilitating visa for business and tourism. Prime Minister Modi has announced that India will issue business visa for 3–5 years for SAARC nations. In fact at the 3rd BIMSTEC summit held in Myanmar in March 2014, the leaders of the sub-regional grouping agreed to facilitate travel through the BIMSTEC Business Visa Scheme, a grouping where all the three countries are members. These facilities can be taken advantage of by the three countries to strengthen their economic ties.

Another area where the three countries could cooperate is in disaster management. The Bay of Bengal is known for fierce and frequent tropical cyclones. It may be noted here that under BIMSTEC, India has established the BIMSTEC Weather and Climate Centre at the National Weather Forecasting Centre in Noida to provide weather warnings. Land border management and maritime security is yet another domain where the three countries could work together for mutual benefits. Today, there are bilateral arrangements to enhance border security and maritime security. Given the nature of the security threats that transcends national borders affecting and endangering peace and stability of the entire region, it is an opportune time for the three countries to cooperate in this area.

## Conclusion

All the three countries are members of several regional and sub-regional groupings such as BIMSTEC. The leaders of the three neighbours could use these existing platforms to further enhance their common interests through meetings on the sidelines of the summits of these forums. India and Bangladesh can tap the new opportunities that are being presented as a result of Myanmar's opening up, while India and Myanmar need to take full advantage of Dhaka's economic outreach. On the other hand, Bangladesh and Myanmar can leverage India's renewed focus on its neighbourhood and the new ideas in Delhi's foreign policy including the growing role and involvement of the states in regional diplomacy where the whole of eastern Indian states, both continental and maritime, could play a role. This is an opportunity for India to take the initiative for a trilateral cooperation ahead. It need not be a major project but even agreeing to link the countries using the connectivity projects that are underway will itself inspire more innovative and bigger projects in the future. In fact by extending the Bangladesh, Bhutan, India, Nepal (BBIN) motor vehicle arrangement to include Myanmar could be a good start.

NOTES

1. "Myanmar's Rohingya Crisis", *IRIN* News, 16 November 2012, at http://www.irinnews.org/report/96801/briefing-myanmar-s-rohingya-crisis
2. "Rakhine Violence Sparks Concern", 12 June, 2012 at http://www.irinnews.org/report/95631/myanmar-rakhine-violence-sparks-concern
3. "Bangladesh Prime Minister Holds Discussions with Myanmar Leaders", *Press Release*, Ministry of Foreign Affairs, Government of Bangladesh, 4 March, 2014 at http://www.mofa.gov.bd/PressRelease/PrintPRDetails.php?txtUserId=&PRid=757
4. "Myanmar's Positive Nod", *The Daily* Star, 9 February, 2015 at http://www.thedailystar.net/myanmars-positive-nod-63883
5. "Myanmar Set to Build Hydropower Plants Targeting Bangladesh", 9 February 2010 at http://www.power-eng.com/articles/2010/09/myanmar-set-to-build.html
6. "A Fresh Move Made to Build Bangladesh-Myanmar Road", *The Financial*

*Express*, 11 April, 2015 at http://www.thefinancialexpress-bd.com/2015/04/11/88436

7. See the full text of Prime Minister Modi's speech at the 18th SAARC Summit in Khatmandu, 26-27 November, 2014 at http://www.narendramodi.in/text-of-prime-ministers-speech-at-2014-saarc-summit-in-nepal
8. Ibid.
9. Farooq Sobhan, "41 Years in the Making", *The Indian Express*, 12 May , 2015 at http://indianexpress.com/article/opinion/columns/india-bangladesh-land-boundary-agreement-41-years-in-the-making
10. "Dispute Concerning Delimitation of the Maritime Boundary between Bangladesh and Myanmar in the Bay of Bengal", International Tribunal for the Law of the Sea, 14 March, 2012 at https://www.itlos.org/fileadmin/itlos/documents/cases/case_no_16/1-C16_Judgment_14_02_2012.pdf
11. "UN Tribunal Fixes Indo-Bangladesh Maritime Border", 9 July, 2014 at http://indianexpress.com/article/india/india-others/un-tribunal-fixes-indo-bangladesh-maritime-border
12. For a discussion on the emerging geopolitics in the Bay of Bengal see David Brewster, "The Rise of the Bengal Tigers: The Growing Strategic Importance of the Bay of Bengal", *Journal of Defence Studies*, Vol. 9, Issue 2, April-June 2015, pp. 81-104; also see K. Yhome, "Myanmar and the Geopolitics of the Bay of Bengal", *Issue Brief* #68, Observer Research Foundation, January 2014 at http://www.observerindia.com/cms/export/orfonline/modules/issuebrief/attachments/issuebrief68_1392022323312.pdf
13. See "*Annual Report 2014: Piracy And Armed Robbery Against Ships In Asia*", ReCAAP Information Sharing Centre, p. 12 at http://www.recaap.org/Portals/0/docs/Reports/2014/ReCAAP%20ISC%20Annual%20Report%202014.pdf
14. "At Least 20 Dead in Bay of Bengal Pirate Attack", *The Maritime Executive*, 2 April, 2013 at http://www.maritime-executive.com/article/At-Least-20-Dead-in-Bay-of-Bengal-Pirate-Attack-2013-04-02
15. "8 Fishermen Injured by Bullets in Bay", *The Financial* Express, 17 February, 2015 at http://www.thefinancialexpress-bd.com/2015/02/17/81603
16. See Anurug Chakma, "Maritime Piracy in Bangladesh", *International Policy Digest*, 24 June, 2014 at http://www.internationalpolicydigest.org/2014/06/24/maritime-piracy-bangladesh. Also see "Risk Assessment: Chittagong, Bangladesh Piracy Threats", *Enodo Global* at http://enodoglobal.com/wp-content/uploads/Enodo_6M-Chittagong_Moheshkali-Piracy-Risk-Assessment_AUG2014-v.2-SPREAD.pdf
17. "Myanmar Navy seeks Arms from India", *The New Indian Express*, 30 July, 2013 at http://www.newindianexpress.com/nation/Myanmar-Navy-seeks-arms-from-India/2013/07/30/article1708731.ece
18. In an earlier paper, this author has argued on similar lines. See K. Yhome, "The Bay of Bengal at the Crossroad: Potential for Cooperation among Bangladesh, India and Myanmar", *FES India Paper*, October 2014 at http://library.fes.de/pdf-files/bueros/indien/11043.pdf
19. See for instance, Richard H. Ullman, "Trilateralism: "Partnership" for What?",

*Foreign Affairs*, October 1976 Issue at http://www.foreignaffairs.com/articles/26598/richard-h-ullman/trilateralism-partnership-for-what

20. Terence P. Stewart & Margaret L.H. Png, "The Growth Triangle of Singapore, Malaysia and Indonesia", *Georgia Journal of International and Comparative Law*, Vol. 23, no. 1, 1993 at http://digitalcommons.law.uga.edu/cgi/viewcontent.cgi?article=1500&context=gjicl
21. See for instance P.K. Ghosh, "Maritime Security Trilateralism: India, Sri Lanka and the Maldives", *Strategic Analysis*, Vol. 38, Issue 3, pp. 283-88.
22. "NSA Level Meeting on Trilateral Maritime Security Cooperation between India, Sri Lanka and Maldives", *Press Release*, Ministry of External Affairs, Government of India, 6 March, 2014 at http://www.mea.gov.in/press-releases.htm?dtl/23037/NSA+level+meeting+on+trilateral+Maritime+Security+Cooperation+between+ India+Sri+Lanka+and+Maldives
23. "Indian Ocean Security Pact Signed", *The Hindu*, 9 July, 2013 at http://www.thehindu.com/news/international/south-asia/indian-ocean-security-pact-signed/article4898042.ece

# 6

# North-East Region: Connecting India and Myanmar

*Sayantani Sen Majumdar*

India's Look East Policy (LEP) is a substantive manifestation of India's renewed emphasis on reviving cooperative ties with its South East Asian neighbours as well as the necessity to reassess India's geopolitical position in the rapidly changing global scenario in the post-Cold War era. The LEP inherits both political and economic implications of the larger policy framework associated with liberalisation, privatisation and globalisation.[1] Phase 2 of the LEP pre-eminently emphasises the development of its North-East Region (NER) because of its geographic, demographic, political, economic, cultural and religious proximity to South East Asia (SEA). NER of India, being peripheral to the South East Asian nations, possesses prospects for potential economic development for the region itself and for the entire country as well.

NER bears a direct surface connection with SEA either through Bangladesh or Myanmar. The inclusion of Myanmar as one of the member countries of the Association of South East Asian Nations (ASEAN) in the year 1997 accords an extra momentum to India's NER policy. India and Myanmar share about a 1,643 km long border and India's cooperation with Myanmar is vital if the potentiality of cross-border region building between the NER and its eastern neighbours is rejuvenated.[2] Geographically, SEA starts with Myanmar and India could not afford to alienate its first potential port of entry into Asia. Myanmar's strategically important geographic location is crucial to its economic relations with India. A benign neglect followed by an outright hostility to the military regime characterised the Indian policy for a fairly long time. The political upheavals in the country hardly had any influence on India's foreign policy pursuits with Myanmar. The political transition in Myanmar from 2011 onwards actually remodelled the contours of India–Myanmar relations to a great extent. The election in 2015 in Myanmar perhaps bears intense implication for their bilateral cooperation. In this context, India's NER might act as an opportune facilitator. To realise the objectives of cooperation with SEA, India pioneered sub-regional initiatives like the Bay of Bengal Initiative for Multi-Sectoral Technical and Economic Cooperation (BIMSTEC) and the Mekong–Ganga Cooperation with Myanmar as the geographical axis for these new undertakings.

The relevance of the NER geography in promoting the India–Myanmar cooperation is the thrust of the analysis of this study as the Indian interests in Myanmar can be summarised by the following considerations:

- Containment of Chinese economic and strategic influences in South East Asia in general and Myanmar in particular.
- Guiding Myanmar in exploring its vibrant gas fields and exploiting the energy resources.
- Getting the Myanmar government to come down heavily on the North-Eastern insurgents and rebel groups that have taken shelter and been pursuing violent activities there.
- To obtain inter-modal transit facility for goods and services being traded between India and South East Asian countries.

## Initiatives and Projects

There lies an extensive possibility for the NER to be a potential beneficiary of India's LEP primarily in two significant ways. The region enjoys an ample scope to gain if the trade is conducted over land across the region. The region has the prospect to benefit directly from it through enhancement of its proportion in the commodity composition in the thriving markets of SEA besides enjoying its direct spill-over effects. Secondly, the LEP can also promote the region, if it is oriented towards invocation and emphasis of the geographical and cultural continuities between South Asia and SEA by encouraging people-to-people contacts across the international borders.[3] Export will boom due to certain favourable factors like low tariffs, collaborative pacts, agreements and Free Trade Agreements. India has pioneered a number of infrastructure projects providing impetus to the political, economic and strategic aspects of the LEP where the onus is on the development of its landlocked NER. Some of the important India–ASEAN projects can be evaluated in terms of their effectiveness in furthering India's LEP. Among the notable joint initiatives undertaken in this aspect is the ASEAN–India Car Rally of 2004, deserving special mention. It was a decisive endeavour undertaken by the Indian government to focus on the geographic proximity between North-East India and SEA. The rally, flagged off from Guwahati, travelled through Myanmar, Thailand, Laos, Vietnam, Cambodia, Malaysia and Singapore over a period of 20 days, before concluding at Batam, Indonesia, on December 11, 2004.[4] The then Indian Prime Minister, Dr Manmohan Singh referred to India's North-East as the gateway to the 'Asian Century' while inaugurating the Asian Car Rally. This rally upholds the credibility of the NER to be the commercial corridor of India linking the ASEAN nations and by enabling its people to harness their economic well-being through trade, transit and tourism. The success of the Car Rally event of 2004 inspired the flagging of another Car Rally venture in December 2012 from Guwahati. In addition to the Car Rally, India has undertaken considerable bilateral and multilateral projects for promoting connectivity between the NER and SEA. The orientation has successfully advanced from 'Look' to 'Link' East. The important ongoing and potential infrastructure projects in this regard are the Moreh-Tamu-Kalewa Road, India-Myanmar-Thailand Trilateral Highway, Trans-Asian Highway, India–Myanmar rail linkages, Kaladan Multimodal project, Stilwell road, Myanmar-India- Bangladesh gas or oil pipeline, Tamanthi Hydroelectricity project and the optical fibre-network between North- East India and South East Asia.[5]

## India-Myanmar-Thailand Trilateral Highway

The Trilateral Highway project is a somewhat ambitious endeavour, which was initially undertaken under the initiatives of the Mekong Ganga Cooperation (MGC) and later shifted to the transport sector of the BIMSTEC but till date it has not yielded any positive outcome. With the motive to commence the project in early 2004, the construction of the 1,360 km highway at the cost of $700 million was divided into three phases so as to connect Moreh (India), Mae Sot (Thailand) through Bagan in Myanmar. The motto behind the construction of the road was to serve the cardinal purpose of establishing a connection between North-East India and SEA. The project unfortunately has faced multiple problems along with acute financial constraints. India and Thailand have upgraded some of the link roads but due to lack of adequate funds in Myanmar, much work remains incomplete. Tensions have also flared up due to Myanmar's demand for India and Thailand taking up the responsibility of bearing the costs of road construction in its territory. Moreover, there are certain crippling security issues in the region. The most crucial are the problems in the India–Myanmar border regions, which are often severely afflicted by hazards like illegal trade, drug trafficking and insurgencies.

Another tension has cropped up with China's overarching control over the Kachin state bordering the Indian state of Arunachal Pradesh, which China claims as its territory and it is apprehended that the commencement of the Trilateral Highway could flood the state with Chinese goods and illegal weapons thereby hampering the security interests of India. Those have always been concerning factors for India but the prospects of accruing long-term benefits from the highways are significant for India, especially for securing its foothold in Myanmar. For India, however, the realisation of the Trilateral Highway will be a bag of mixed opportunities. The Trilateral project raises concern on its final destination, that is the Myanmar–Thailand border, where the ethnic insurgent camps are still in existence. Myanmar, in the past had been sceptical of Thailand for safeguarding groups like the Karen National Union and the Chin National Liberation Front.

The cross-border infrastructure has also been hindered due to Thailand's apprehension about the negative impact of the steady inflow of illegal immigrants and the rampant narcotic business. Apart from all these practical impediments on the pursuit of the Trilateral Highway, the presence of profound tenets of regionalism could also be cited as a considerable reason for the delay. For instance, the quicker integration of the Greater Mekong Sub region (GMS) has often overshadowed the performance of other regional organisations like the BIMSTEC and the MGC. While cross-border connectivity has been boosted between the GMS countries, it has considerably eroded the scope of the projects like the Trilateral Highway as the Mekong region countries are increasingly getting trapped in the economic clutches of China.

Presently the GMS countries' concentration is on the construction and the upgradation of new highways under the Asian Highway Project and already approximately $2.7 billion have been invested into this initiative.[6] The East West Corridor, the North-South Economic Corridor and the Southern Economic Corridor are the three major projects being administered here. The development of these highways and ratification of the Cross Border Transport Agreement (CBTA) have since quadrupled the intra-GMS trade. It is appalling to notice the inadequacy of the Trilateral Highway initiatives due to severe political and financial incongruities. It is highly expected that the completion of the Trilateral Highway will promote greater connectivity between India and South East Asia and the positives will inevitably outweigh the negatives in every sense. Connectivity will certainly open up new vistas of cooperation with the neighbouring states and this will provide effective mechanisms for dealing with cross-border problems which hitherto have remained unresolved. Additionally, since the Trilateral Highway will connect India to the Asian Highway Network, the prospect of booming trade between India and ASEAN is quite high. This will accelerate the trade potentialities of India, Myanmar and Thailand which are mostly maritime in nature. Moreover, India's NER will function as a competent hub of trade and commerce.[7]

Recent media reports communicate that Myanmar and Thailand have made considerable headway in their parts to promote this Highway but the lacunae lies in the case of India as there are certain political issues claiming immediate attention. Therefore, India needs to be more proactive in implementing this project since considerable progress from its counterparts, Thailand and Myanmar, has been made and India needs to catch up.

## The Moreh-Tamu-Kalewa Road

There are two or more semi-official border crossings between India and Myanmar, which can be used by the locals only. One of them is from Tamu on the Myanmarese side to Moreh (*Morei*) in Manipur on the Indian side. India in its quest to stimulate its LEP, and Thailand for the purpose of boosting trade, aims to upgrade this route and enhance commerce between the two countries. India has even upgraded the road from Tamu to Kalewa, about 150 kilometres inside Myanmar. But due to major shortcomings like the spiralling problem of insurgency, poor infrastructure, preference of sea route over land routes, the influence of various pressure groups, frequent bandhs and blockades, overarching uncertainties among the trading communities, the absence of proper electricity supply, telephone, internet and the banking system in the Moreh–Tamu area, the route from India to Thailand through Myanmar is far from real.

The border area is the fulcrum of illegal transactions. The practical scenario is that there is no concrete land route between India and Thailand and no viable land—or water—route between India and its strategically significant neighbour, Myanmar.[8] At the diplomatic level, the arrival of the then Minister of External Affairs, Shri Jaswant Singh, in Myanmar in a visit from February 13–15, 2001, marked an imprint on India's Myanmar Policy. The momentous angle of this visit was the fact that the Indian delegation went to Myanmar by road for the first time.[9] On February 13, 2001, Shri Jaswant Singh, along with the Myanmarese military officials, inaugurated the only legal border custom post opened along the 1,643 km long common border.

The city of Moreh got connected to the Myanmarese city of Tamu (Sagaing Division).[10] India financed the construction of 160 kilometres of the road leaving Tamu towards Mandalay, which ends in Kalewa while Myanmar was entrusted with the responsibility of planning and undertaking the construction of the rest of the road.[11] The Rs 90-crore road built by India's Border Road Organisation was India's gift to Myanmar. While inaugurating the road, in his speech, the honourable minister said: 'the natural movement of goods, people and services for the North- East is not through Calcutta" and he described the importance of "opening up the natural outlet of the North-East".[12]

The project received a breakthrough in April 2002, when Shri Jaswant Singh again visited Myanmar to meet both the Myanmarese military representatives and the Thai officials who were intensely interested in the construction of a commercial route linking India with Indochina via Mandalay in Myanmar. The highway project linking the countries was signed on April 6, 2002 in Yangon. But, unfortunately the project has not yet been implemented and the financing remains highly hypothetical.[13] A strong political will and determination of all the three countries are the basic prerequisites for the steady implementation of the project.

It is often alleged that Myanmar is one of the focal drug-trafficking centres in the world.[14] And, most of the ethnic and political insurgents in the NER and Myanmar are widely involved in the drug -trafficking network. There is a dearth of reliable data on the drug routes from western Myanmar to NER and Bangladesh, whereas the drug framework in northern Myanmar is quite popular. India is also a producer of caffeine and ephedrine as well as of codeine—products that are exported to Myanmar. The processed drugs are routed to Kolkata and Cox's Bazar (the Bangladesh port). Since the late 1990s, this Indian route for drugs from Myanmar has expanded further, flooding the NER. The Indian and Myanmarese authorities lack the competence to control this menace and are often accused of being ignorant about the outcomes of these heinous activities involving drug-trafficking and money-laundering transactions.[15] The India–Myanmar Road has become a priority for India's diplomacy.[16] With the addition of the Thai project, which also intends to establish a link through road by connecting Mandalay to the Thai border, Myanmar and especially the city of Mandalay could well become a major hub of terrestrial trade flows between South Asia, China and SEA.[17]

## Tamanthi Hydroelectric Project

Gauging the inherent significance of the project, India undertook the initiative to rejuvenate the stalled 1,200MW Tamanthi Hydroelectric power plant and the 642MW Shwezaye project on the Chindwin River, the largest tributary of the Irrawaddy River, Myanmar's key commercial waterway. The Memorandum of Association for these projects is in the process of getting signed and is making considerable headway. This momentous undertaking is undoubtedly an indication of India's quest to cultivate diplomatic and economic ties with its resource-rich neighbour. Myanmar is rich in resources particularly hydrocarbon reserves, which can be of great importance for India's energy security. India ranks among the top 10 largest oil-consuming countries. Myanmar has the world's 10$^{th}$ largest natural gas reserves, estimated at over 90 trillion cubic feet in 19 onshore and the three major offshore fields. Myanmar has natural gas reserves of 89.722 trillion cu. ft (tcf), of which 18.012 tcf are proven recoverable reserves, or gas that can be easily extracted and tapped.[18] Tamanthi is in north Myanmar. Once completed, the project is expected to control floods and provide water for irrigation in the region. India would be the recipient of the bulk of the power generated. Myanmar has a hydroelectric power potential of 39,720MW and an installed capacity of 747MW. A power transmission link with Myanmar would also help towards a power inter-link of the countries of the South Asian Association for Regional Cooperation (SAARC) which groups India, Pakistan, Nepal, Bhutan, Myanmar, Bangladesh, Sri Lanka, Afghanistan and the Maldives. Appraising the utility of the project, the SAARC grid has envisaged the meeting of electricity demands and in reinvigorating the economic and political ties in the region. These projects are integral to India's engagement with Myanmar.[19]

## Stilwell Road

Arunachal Pradesh is an isolated state in North-East India awaiting an opening and an historic route like Stilwell. Debates and dialogues are on the surface on the pros and cons of reopening of the Stilwell Road and several efforts have been undertaken in this respect. This historic road connects the three backward regions of the NER, northern Myanmar and south-west China. It emanates from Assam and links Kunming in the Yunnan Province of South-West China through the Pangsau Pass of the India-Myanmar border. This land route which was rebuilt during World War II was used for cross-regional movement between the contiguous regions of India, Myanmar and China for various purposes. It was known by various names like the Ledo Road, Burma Road and the Bhamo Road which was extensively used for various trans-regional movements.

The Road was in full use for more than one and a half years for emergency purposes and military transport but after the independence of India and Myanmar, it was closed for security reasons though unofficial movements still exist. This meandering path which connects three close neighbours of this region with 61 kilometres lying in Indian territory, 1,033 kilometres within Myanmar and the remaining 633 kilometres within China, got truncated and lost momentum due to the changed geopolitical realities of the region.

A fresh thought is now being given to this Road as a potential passage for the socio-economic development of this contiguous region. The border region of the Patkai range is still inhabited by a dozen ethnic communities and an opening up of this Road will help to connect them and restore the links lost ethnically and culturally across the border. To them, the reopening of the Stilwell Road is like a dream come true. Among the three nations through which the Road runs, China has already pursued the idea of reopening and has repelled the idea of the constructive stretch of the Road with the 6 Link Express Highway. But, Myanmar has been extremely indecisive regarding the reopening as it passes through the jungle-covered mountainous and swampy valley of the Kachin state—the most insurgency-prone area. India has also been in an uncomfortable position. However, there has been a ray of hope as Myanmar has agreed to honour the long-standing need of the region by reopening the Stilwell Road to facilitate trade with India, China and Myanmar. For the NER, the Road makes it possible to use Myanmar for channellising its goods to the ASEAN countries. The Stilwell road is expected to cut 30 percent transport cost between India and China, thereby boosting Sino-Indian overland trade.

Cargoes can then reach Yunnan in two days instead of two weeks. Most importantly, the otherwise isolated state of Arunachal Pradesh would be connected to Myanmar. Apart from trade, it would also be used to tap the untapped resources like horticulture, floriculture and tourism. It is meant for reviving the closed cultural, spiritual and ethnic ties but the NER should not be used as a dumping ground for Chinese products. There should be good intra-regional understanding for the reopening of the Road through an intra-regional connectivity and there should be appropriate laws, rules, customs regulations and security forces.

China has already completed the construction of its stretch of the Stilwell Road with the only major impediment being the coarse section of the legendary road in Myanmar, which Yangon finds less interested in building up. Myanmar apprehends that the Stilwell Road which passes through its Kachin region, is primarily hassled with militant camps belonging to the outfits from India's North-East Region and hence reopening the Road might provide an easier access to the rebels.[20]

That apprehension might be one of the vital causes behind Myanmar's reluctance to open the Road or in delaying the implementation of the project. In India, the 61 km of the stretch is being shared by Assam and Arunachal Pradesh—30 km lie in Assam and the other 31 km in Arunachal Pradesh. Previously, the border between Assam and Arunachal Pradesh, which has about a 14 km road section, was in a miserable condition but recently it has been rebuilt and renovated and the construction of the international trade route is also underway to connect Myanmar at the Pangsau Pass.

The reopening of the Stilwell Road is being conceived with great expectation as it bears the prospect of making the region a major international trade centre.[21] The NER has been a trouble spot for India due to historical reasons and due to the occurrence of insurgency and other violent activities. Disconnect has kept it in isolation from mainland India and with the close neighbours which share almost 98 percent of the boundaries with the NER. The LEP, conceived of a) rebuilding the lost relations with the fast-growing SEA nations; b) Revival of the landlocked and conflict-prone borderland of NER through its connectivity with the South East Asian nations with Myanmar as a gateway so that it can be conceptualised as a trans-regional economic and cultural space to counter this long-standing issue of insurgency, poverty and economic backwardness.

## Kaladan Multimodal Project

India on April 2, 2008 signed the decade-long Kaladan Multi Modal Transit Transport Project with Myanmar that opened India's access through an alternative route to the North-Eastern states. India is vividly exploring the possibility of harnessing Myanmar's Chindwin River (i.e. the development of hydroelectric capacities that would be eventually redirected towards the Indian North-East) and especially the Kaladan River sector. Flowing from Mizoram to the Rakhine State (Arakan) of Myanmar, this river could be of strategic importance for India as it could enable it to develop a suitable communication route via the East, bypassing Bangladesh. In that perspective, India has offered to upgrade the commercial port of Sittwe (formerly Akyab), where the Kaladan River falls into the Bay of Bengal.

The commercial use of such a harbour could be valuable for India's traders, especially those who are interested in commercial transactions from Kolkata or the Indian eastern coast to the North-East of India but through Myanmar and the Kaladan River instead of going through the Siliguri Neck and Assam. Moreover, a collaboration between the Myanmarese and the Mizoram authorities was necessary for developing Mizoram's system.[22] The project bears the potentiality of developing the Sittwe port on the Kaladan River from where the goods will be transported. The $ 120 million agreement was signed by the Indian Minister of External Affairs, Shri Pranab Mukherjee and his Myanmar counterpart U Nyan Win. The completion of the Kaladan Project is expected to facilitate India an access route from any corner of the country to the NER.

Moreover, the implementation of the project will provide India an alternative trading route thereby diminishing the need of transition through Bangladesh. Besides developing the ports, the project is oriented to construct and develop a road linking Kalewa in Myanmar to Moreh, the border town in the NER of India, at an estimated cost of INR 5.3 billion.[23] India needs to have a developed and modernised Myanmar as its neighbour, equipped with an effective infrastructure, especially if it wishes to see its NER opened up and developed. The economic expansion of the region should not end at its border, but should also include other regions, the Indian NER, Bangladesh and Western Myanmar.[24]

India is equally keen to develop Myanmar's energy resources. An offshore natural gas deposit facing the Arakan coast is being developed by two Indian companies in cooperation with two Korean companies (Daewoo International with a share of 60 percent; Korea Gas Corporation with a share of 10 percent; Gas Authority of India Ltd with 10 percent and the Oil and Natural Gas Corporation—ONGC Videsh—with a share of 20 percent).[25] The pipeline project for linking the Arakan deposit to Bangladesh and Kolkata could not be implemented as yet because of Bangladesh's reluctance to go ahead with the project. The visit of the Myanmarese leader, senior General Than Shwe, to India on July, 2010, sparked a new excitement for India's LEP signalling decisive progress in the context of physical connectivity between India's North- East and Myanmar—an advanced step in the LEP. After the Kaladan Multimodal Transport System, India has announced the building of yet another new road, the Rhi–Tiddim and Rhi–Falam road connecting Mizoram to Myanmar. The next stage of feasibility on the Tamanthi Hydel Project is also being discussed. India is proceeding carefully on this 1200 MW project on river Chindwin in north-western Myanmar. Moreover, India has decided to grant $10 million for agricultural implements for Myanmar's farmers and boost telecommunication links by strengthening the optic-fibre link with microwave. India will assist with an extra $ 60 million for railway upgradation.[26]

## Conclusion

The NER is endowed with immense potentialities but what is needed is the proper harnessing of the production capacities and surpluses. One of the prime motives of the LEP is to generate revenue from the East. For meeting this end, India has to steer the strategy of positioning the surpluses and the capacities in the international markets and imbibing them with the required market power thereby strengthening the market presence. The qualities of the NER need to be showcased. Each state is blessed with a typical characteristic of its own and it should specialise in that unique feature to market it internationally. This will eventually accelerate economic growth and the NER will reap economic benefits from trade. In order to accomplish this, there should be synergy and coordinated efforts between the Central and the State governments.

The Central Government has opted for granting huge amount of funds for the progress of the region. The region suffers from basic structural inefficiency. There is no accountability on public expenditure and the lack of the responsiveness of the people impedes the harnessing of abundant economic potentials ultimately shaking the prospect of a better future for the region.[27] Transparency, accountability along with proper and timely execution of the projects should be the guiding spirit of the LEP. Prime Minister Modi's 2015 Bangladesh visit will stimulate the connectivity cooperation between the two neighbours wherein the NER of India has a lot to benefit. We know that the opening of India to SEA is mainly through two countries, namely Bangladesh and Myanmar. Therefore promoting the connectivity initiative is a key aspect on the agenda of bilateral cooperation. A milestone in this endeavour is the initiative for the road linkages between Bangladesh, Bhutan, India and Nepal (BBIN). Once implemented, transportation will take place and vehicles from all the four countries will be directed to transit goods across each other's territories via the transport corridors. This launch is going to add momentum to trade and commerce as well as business opportunities thereby rejuvenating people-to-people contacts. Moreover, India will be gaining easy access to its NER as transit through Bangladesh will decrease the travel time. The proposed Kolkata-Dhaka-Agartala and Guwahati-Shillong-Dhaka bus service bears much credence. The BBIN can boost up regional integration but an infrastructural development is required. India needs to comprehend the relevance of its geostrategic location and potential and it can be as decisive as China's Silk Road Economic Belt in substantiating the creation of a conducive ecosystem, liberalised visas, easy trade permits and smooth conduction of trade thereby revitalising regional growth by opening overland access to Bangladesh, Myanmar, Thailand, Malaysia and beyond. Moreover, Modi's visit to Bangladesh may strengthen India's integration with its North-East as well as SEA particularly in the backdrop of the India–Bangladesh relations which are in need of transformation and modification for the strategic advantages of both the neighbours. This is a decisive drive for India's Act East Policy.

Despite all the developmental initiatives and strengthening of bilateral ties with Myanmar, India still considers China's influence on Myanmar as a challenging proposition.[28] Whether or not Myanmar's historical trajectories would be influencing its future discourses, depend a lot on the intersecting and interfering factors. If the political and economic transformations are being properly installed and institutionalised, the parallel socio-cultural changes are likely to follow. Though there are influences of India and China as neighbours on Myanmar's socio-economic and political track, still Myanmar's future will be shaped by its own past, historical patterns, own human and material contexts and own beliefs and it would not be dictated by anyone else's terms and conditions. Indeed Myanmar's priorities will be agrarian and domestic; its government will be a centralised hybrid of primarily indigenous and foreign ideas and realities of the foreseeable future, its past will continue to be an indelible part of its present.[29] President Thein Shein has adopted proactive measures to erase the identification of the country as the poorest cousin of its South East Asian neighbours. But, India's LEP has rendered an added impetus to the India–Myanmar relations which have been reinvigorated by the exchange of visits from both the neighbours. It is noteworthy to mention that from 2011 onwards, after Myanmar's transition to democracy, the relations are getting warmer. Myanmar has witnessed marked changes in its domestic policies and actions as well as security issues and foreign policy issues. Reforming the electoral system, releasing the political prisoners, encouraging media freedom, expanding civil society groups, establishing a national human rights commission and a peace-building institute are some hallmarks of the new Myanmar, which to some extent, have bewildered the international community. There are certain predominant aspects like reunification, restoration of identity, self-reliance and return to identity that have been identified as still being crucial to the development trajectory of Myanmar. The Rohingya issue is playing a major role in the India–Myanmar bilateral chemistry. India has been 'a friend in need' in Myanmar's time of distress and might provide an example to other countries to take up the initiative to help ease the plight of this immensely deplorable community.[30] There is also considerable scope for India to assume a vital role in changing the political, economic and strategic future of Myanmar. The Myanmarese officials believe that a futuristic course of India–Myanmar relations would be determined and redefined by the level of India's cooperation and its encouraging contribution to the country's process of modernisation. That in turn, will reveal India's renewed concerns about the independence and autonomy of Myanmar thereby reinforcing its own security interests.

In the complex strategic context of the Myanmarese politics, taking cognisance of Myanmar's resource-richness and international dynamics, the US, China and Japan have been enthusiastically outlining their strategic priorities and requirements in the country. Their extensive engagements should incite India to strengthen its age-old connections with Myanmar. India needs to reorient the grand design of developing the NER like China's Western Development Strategy of transforming Yunnan into a world-class destination. The development of border trade mandates a differential advantage from the NER of producing quality goods at competitive costs using own resources of the region. It has already been argued earlier that the knowledge and command over English language by the North-Eastern people can facilitate the pace of cooperation with Myanmar over China. But, there should be consensus among all the eight North-Eastern states and a collective plan of action is the need of the hour. Proper synchronisation of the policies of the Central Government and the State Governments are imperative to make the NER the harbinger of thriving cooperation between the neighours—India and Myanmar. India must deepen its ties with its neighbour by its soft power diplomacy and Track II initiatives wherein education, culture, democracy can play an effective and enduring role by leveraging such comparative advantages to build interdependence and mutual benefits contributing to peace and stability in SEA and East Asia.

## NOTES

1. Hanjabam Gyanendro Sharma, "Look East Policy: The Gaze and its Dangers in the North East" in *Alternative Frames,* Centre for Alternative Discourse, Manipur, 2006, p.80.
2. Sanjib Baruah, *Durable Disorder: Understanding the Politics of Northeast India*, New Delhi, Oxford University Press, 2005, p.224.
3. Samir Das, '"Between South and Southeast Asia: Recasting India's Northeast in the Age of Globalisation" in Asok Kumar Ray and Satyabrata Chakraborty (eds.) *Society Politics and Development in North East India,* New Delhi, Concept Publishing Company, 2008, pp. 151,152.
4. Accessed electronically from (*www.tatamotors.com/our_world/press_releases.php?ID)* on 26.10.09.

5. Julien Levesque, "North East in India's Look East Policy", *Institute of Peace and Conflict Studies*, New Delhi, May 6, 2008, accessed electronically from (http://www.ipcs.org/articles_details.php?articleNo=2558$cID=9) on 15.10.09.
6. Accessed electronically from (*www.indoburmanews.net/.../india-myanmar-thailand-trilateral-highway/)* on 09.07.10.
7. Accessed electronically from (*www.indoburmanews.net/.../india-myanmar-thailand-trilateral-highway/)* on 10.07.10.
8. Accessed electronically from (*pad16.com/sea_broken/myanmar/**burmaroad**.htm)* on 15.06.10.
9. "A Rewarding Visit, Says Jaswant", *The Hindu*, February 15, 2001
10. "Myanmar shows India the Road to Southeast Asia", *Asia Times*, February 21, 2001.
11. "India's Road to Rangoon", *BBC South Asia News*, February 14, 2001.
12. *Assam Tribune*, 2001.
13. "Green Light for Pan-Asia Road Scheme", *BBC South Asia News*, April 6, 2002.
14. "1000 Acres of Poppy Fields Destroyed in Myanmar", *The Times of India*, March 22, 2002.
15. "In a Vicious Circle", *Frontline*, Volume 19, Issue 15, July-August, 2002.
16. "The Roads to Myanmar", *Frontline*, Volume 18, Issue 05, March, 2001.
17. *BBC South Asia News*, April 6, 2002.
18. "Myanmar: Open for Business", accessed electronically from (*www.hfw.com/publications/client.../myanmar-open-for-business)* on 19.02.13.
19. Accessed electronically from (www.info.shine.com/Article/Power/Indian...to...projects/...cid948.aspx) on 9.07.10.
20. Accessed electronically fromt (*www.thaindian.com/.../myanmar-says-no-to-reopening-stilwell-road-plan-shelved_100206308.html)* on 19.06.10.
21. Accessed electronically fromt (www. *changlang.nic.in/stilwell.html)* on 19.06.10.
22. Renaud Egreteau, *Wooing The Generals: India's New Burma Policy*, New Delhi, Authorspress, 2003, p.161.
23. Accessed electronically from (*kaladan.com/kaladan-project/kaladan-mmtt-project/)* on 29.06.10.
24. Subhash Kapila, "India-Myanmar Strategic Partnership: Indian Imperatives", Paper 197, *South Asia Analysis Group*, February 6, 2001.
25. "ONGC Plans to Invest Rs 2900 Crores in North East", *The Hindu*, July 21, 2002.
26. Indrani Bagchi, "Gen Visit to Deepen Ties with Myanmar", *The Times of India*, September 26, 2012.
27. Ibid.
28. J. Mohan Malik, "Myanmar's Role in Regional Security: Pawn or Pivot?' *Contemporary Southeast Asia*, Volume 19, Number 1, Institute of South East Asian Studies, June, 1997, p.56.
29. Michael Aung-Thwin and Maitrii Aung-Thwin (eds.), *A History of Myanmar Since Ancient Times: Traditions and Transformations*, London, Reakton Books Ltd, 2012.
30. Salman Haider, "A Drift on Open Waters", *The Statesman*, Kolkata, May 26, 2015.

# 7

# China and Myanmar's Elections: *plus ça change, plus c'est la même chose*?

*Jabin T. Jacob*

Myanmar's decision to conduct its first general elections under military rule and for its military to willingly start giving up some of its influence and authority in the country's political and economic life—though still only in a limited fashion—has a number of implications for China. With Myanmar's second general elections of November 2015, it is important to examine what impact Myanmar's transition to electoral 'democracy' has for China and how China might itself seek to act in response to that transition. This paper argues that while there are some changes that are evident in Myanmar's external opportunities because of its political transition, China continues to maintain a fair degree of influence in the country both through traditional methods as well as innovation in its own foreign policy.

## Myanmar's Elections and their Impact on China: Of Learning and Ideology

The Communist Party of China (CPC) is a great learner. Following the fall of the Soviet Union, the CPC undertook a serious self-examination. It sought to understand both the reasons for the failure of the CPSU and the secret to why some political parties managed to stay in power for so long. Thus, it was that the CPC began bilateral exchanges with political parties from across the world. Of particular interest were the Partido

Revolucionario Institucional (Institutional Revolutionary Party, PRI) in Mexico and the Congress (I) in India both of which were among the longest-ruling political parties in the world and in power until quite recently. And these exchanges continue. The CPC also had frequent meetings not just with the Communist Party of India-Marxist (CPI-M) in India but also with the Bharatiya Janata Party (BJP) when it was in the opposition. Now that the BJP is in power, these linkages have also become more intense and multifaceted.

To come to the case of Myanmar, there are at least three ways in which China is affected by developments in a Myanmar that goes to the polls in 2015. One, it will seek to learn from the Myanmarese experience and adopt such measures as might be useful to itself; two, it might view certain developments as threatening its national interests and three, it will try to contextualise Myanmar's developments in terms of China's own political concepts and ideology.

*China Learns*

China calls itself a democracy and is technically also a multiparty system—the Chinese People's Political Consultative Conference (CPPCC), which is one of the two national-level advisory bodies in the state, for instance, has in addition to the CPC, eight other political parties that constitute the United Front. It is also important to note that 'democracy' and 'political parties' are not mere labels in China but subjects and concepts of intense debate and discussion. True, the parameters are restricted, and the number of participants limited to a literate, educated, technologically-savvy population—but it is also the case that the Chinese leaders have to take into account the general mood of the people in their policymaking.[1]

Further, the 'rule of law' was the major theme of the Fourth Plenum of the 18th Central Committee of the CPC held in October 2014, though even here it might be better described as 'rule by law' or 'rule according to law' (*yi fa zhiguo*) than 'rule of law'. China's own equivalent of a Lower House of Parliament, the National People's Congress (consisting only of members of the CPC) as well as the upper house equivalent, the CPPCC, have both been increasingly assertive in their dealings with the government and on creating and pushing legislation.

In other words, what Myanmar is experimenting with is also being studied and experimented with by the Chinese and there are, no doubt, lessons that are being drawn from Myanmar's path and progress. Indeed, this activity has over time displayed greater sophistication and nuance in China's dealings by extending its contacts to the various political parties and civil society organisations in the country even as the Chinese maintain their ties with the Myanmarese military and continues high-level political visits to the country.[2]

*Dangerous Ideas?*

There are however, certain elements of Myanmar's transition that probably are a matter of concern for the CPC. Among these are the matters related to 'federalism' and the role of civil society organisations. There is today a greater openness to federalism within Myanmar, including within its army, as a way of resolving the country's ethnic issues,[3] and there has of course, always been the *Panglong Agreement* in the background. For China, however, 'federalism' based along ethnic lines is a highly sensitive and problematic issue in the context of its restive ethnic minority-dominated provinces such as Tibet and Xinjiang or Inner Mongolia. Beijing has, in fact, expressed its reservations about another neighbour, Nepal, seeking to address the concerns of its minority groups by way of ethnicity-based federalism.[4] In fact, this sort of federalism reflects closely the Indian version of federalism and perhaps, forms or will form another facet of Sino-Indian political/ideological competition. And just as Beijing has tried in Nepal, so also it might in Myanmar, to redirect political reconciliation efforts away from ethnicity-based federalism.

Of course, the level of sensitivity with respect to Nepal is considerably higher than it is with Myanmar. The former borders highly sensitive Tibet and the latter the relatively stable Yunnan. Further, given its long involvement and interactions with Myanmar's various ethnic political organisations and armed groups, one might even argue that any ethnicity-based arrangement, even federalism, might not materially change China's influence and could, in fact, even increase its influence.[5] It remains to be seen if true federalism will come to Myanmar and/or how decentralisation operates in reality in the country.

Coming to the question of the operation of civil society organisations, the CPC has as of now, expressed no desire to give up its hold on power or to share it with other parties. Civil society organisations in China are seen as rivals or counter to the CPC, especially if they were to have a national or cross-regional identity. So, Myanmar's opening up to civil society organisations and the impact it will have for the staying power of the Myanmarese military, will be a matter of some considerable interest in Beijing.

Finally, Chinese media has also been on record expressing concern about religion-inspired political activity and protests in Myanmar. Besides, accusing the Buddhist monks of xenophobia, particularly with respect to the country's Muslim population, an article in the state-owned *Global Times*, referring specifically to the joint Sino-Myanmarese Monywa copper mine project in the Sagaing Region, argued that "the political intervention of monks in Myanmar has significantly worsened the country's investment environment".[6]

*Promoting the China Dream*

There is a still a larger issue at stake for the CPC given the political transitions or the lack thereof, in its neighbourhood: consider the semi-stable democracy in Afghanistan, the somewhat handicapped democracy in Pakistan with the Pakistan Army as a significant political player, the troubled republicanism in Nepal, the constitutional monarchy in Bhutan, the Umbrella Movement Protests in Hong Kong, the record of democratic elections in Taiwan, and the 'disciplined and flourishing democracy' in Myanmar. This is the question of the attractiveness of the Chinese model of political development. Despite claims to non-interference and stepping back from the Maoist era's overt efforts to export the revolution, culturally, China as a civilisation-state and the CPC as a political party cannot but try to put forward a vision of what China wishes the world to look like.

It is in this context that Chinese President Xi Jinping's China Dream concept comes into the picture. This is a concept/ideology that talks of Chinese national rejuvenation[7] but in an interconnected world, Myanmar's elections and the direction of its political transition will affect the China Dream and the content of China's 'national rejuvenation' and vice versa. For instance, Myanmar's President and Speaker have been exchanging letters publicly over their differences,[8] but the equivalent of this would be unheard of in China. Further, the fact that it is the military in Myanmar that has begun the process of political change from its position as rulers of the country might also make an impression on ordinary Chinese people and generate questions about the level of commitment of the CPC to political reform and change.

That said, China's position on Myanmar's elections in particular, or on Myanmar's political transition in general, has to be seen in the light of China's own political transitions of various kinds—and there is political transition in China, even if it might not be visible. It would be a mistake to assume that China has a black-and-white approach of opposition to democratisation in Myanmar.

Beijing will go for whatever works in ensuring that Myanmar remains a stable, peaceful country that provides opportunities for Chinese economic interests to flourish and does not simultaneously create room for non-Asian powers and values. When China supports democracy, it is actually supporting a system that preserves the right of each country to develop a political system suitable to its own 'national conditions'. Thus, when it supports democracy in Afghanistan, for example, it is supporting not specifically the current elected dispensation in Kabul but an 'Afghan people-led' political process; that is, to say, there is scope for the Taliban to come back to power, even if not through elections.[9]

It might also be argued in this context that Beijing is not as worried about India's influence in Myanmar as it has been sensitive to the influence of external powers like the United States of America.

## Chinese Impact on Myanmar: Non-Interference, Really?

Coming to how China might seek to influence Myanmar in its current phase of political transition, one might explain this in terms of China's supposed principle of non-interference in the internal affairs of other countries. While mutual non-interference in internal affairs is a core principle of Chinese foreign policy, the expansion of Chinese enterprises outside its borders does not allow for its easy practice. Chinese interference hitherto has been subtle and difficult to detect because of the tendency for these moves to take place at the level of the political elites and thus away from the public eye. Whether the restarting of the Myitsone dam in Myanmar[10] is a case in point, will require further investigation. But it is perhaps, inevitable that despite claims to being a different sort of world power than the United States, structural conditions—the way the international system is organised, the need to defend the rights and profits of its SOEs and other private enterprises, security interests—will force China to seek to 'guide' outcomes in other countries, including its neighbours, and in increasingly overt ways.

There are, in effect, two kinds of interference that China practices in Myanmar. The traditional or historical methods that it has employed include support for various ethnic insurgencies and of frequent and high-level diplomatic exchanges to get its points of view across. The non-traditional or newer forms of potential 'interference' include the use of new political and economic initiatives such as the new Silk Roads initiative and the Asian Infrastructure Investment Bank (AIIB) to get its points of view across and to convince these countries of the advantages of meeting China's demands.

*Traditional Modes of Interference*

When seven Myanmar soldiers were killed and 20 wounded in an attack by Kokang rebels in the north-eastern frontier with China in early December 2014, the Chinese Foreign Ministry Spokesman was asked about the incident[11] indicating, at the very least, the belief that China continues to back the Kokang and other insurgent groups in Myanmar. The Kokang insurgents, also known as the Myanmar National Democratic Alliance Army (MNDAA), were formerly part of the Communist Party of Burma, a China-backed guerrilla alliance that battled the Myanmar government until it fell apart in 1989. The MNDAA signed a ceasefire agreement with the government that year—the first of about a dozen ethnic armed groups to do so—but in 2009 had clashed with the Myanmarese military that resulted in a serious refugee crisis in the region with tens of thousands of refugees streaming into Yunnan. This incident had also led to a war of words between China and Myanmar at the time.

In March 2015, there were further tensions when as part of Myanmar's action against the Kokang rebels, a village on the Chinese side of the border in Yunnan province was bombed resulting in Chinese casualties.[12] Despite some strong statements within the country,[13] the Chinese side acted with considerable restraint and eventually won an apology from the Myanmarese side.[14] Earlier, the Myanmar Army had claimed that the Kokang rebels had received Chinese arms and even had Chinese mercenaries fighting with them.[15] Such charges have, of course, been denied by Beijing.[16]

High-level visits are frequent between Myanmar and China and offer another opportunity for the Chinese to either state or sell to NayPyitaw exactly what the Chinese interests and demands are. Aside from stressing the need to maintain high-level exchanges and enhance strategic communications, in late 2014, for instance, Chinese Vice-President Li Yuanchao in talks with his Myanmar counterpart U Nyan Tun in the Myanmarese capital said that both sides had to learn from each other's governing experience.[17] Clearly, this is an effort by China to project itself as a role model for Myanmar rather than the other way around. During Premier Li Keqiang's visit to Myanamar in November 2014, in a meeting with Myanmar's Speaker of the Union Parliament and the House of Representatives U Shwe Mann, alongside calls for "joint efforts to propel pragmatic cooperation" and to "enrich the content of China-Myanmar friendship" was also the hope that the two sides could "consolidate the public opinion on the basis of bilateral relations".[18] This is a less than subtle hint to Myanmar to manage its sometimes hostile public opinion on Chinese investment and infrastructure projects. The specific accusations against the protesting Buddhist monks over the Monywa mine project referred to above, is a case in point.

*Interference under the Conditions of 'Win–Win'*

China's new Silk Roads initiative, including a special Silk Roads Fund of some $40 billion and other big-ticket projects like the recently-formed AIIB—of which Myanmar is a member—and before that the Chinese-driven creation of the BRICS New Development Bank, are all designed to parlay its influence across the region in an apparently non-threatening and seemingly non-hegemonic manner. These moves are particularly relevant to Myanmar's circumstances and have implications for its political transition and other developments.

China's infrastructural links with Myanmar are already quite strong and well developed, going beyond just road links from Yunnan and extending to hydroelectric and other projects. But this linkage has always been seen as one, a legacy of ties between two authoritarian states and two, the result of the unequal power relationship between the two countries. The latter aspect, in fact, has probably resulted in Myanmar's constant unease over its ties with China and about taking these too far. The decisive manner of Myanmar's opening up to the outside world—particularly, the West—is, no doubt, partly the result of this overhanging Chinese influence. Even over a decade of the BCIM Regional Cooperation Forum a multilateral programme—albeit a Yunnan-initiated one—did not really allay Myanmar's concerns because India which was concerned about Chinese influence in its politically-sensitive Northeast, moved rather too slowly on bilateral initiatives in Myanmar itself.

China's big new Silk Roads initiative—also known as the 'One Belt, One Road' (*yidai yilu*) project—however, is designed to put all past initiatives in the shade and perhaps aimed to address the problems associated with those initiatives. The 'One Belt, One Road' project is an ambitious multi-country exercise that Beijing claims to seek common development, and is portrayed as being open and inclusive in nature without China seeking a hegemonic role. The BCIM Economic Corridor, proposed by Chinese Premier Li Keqiang during his visit to India in May 2013,[19] will now possibly be subsumed under the land-based part of the new Silk Road. During his visit, the Chinese Vice-President Li Yuanchao also sought to draw Myanmar into the maritime leg known as the 21st Century Maritime Silk Road[20] which no doubt builds on the oil and gas pipelines built from the Myanmarese coast to Yunnan. Together, these initiatives seek to strengthen China's position in Myanmar not just as a special case built on geographical proximity—though this also counts for much—but as a general case of Chinese involvement in that country as in all other countries..[21]

And, since such Chinese presence along the new Silk Roads necessarily involves dealings with countries with different kinds of political systems, Myanmar's transition to 'democracy'—its political system—is not a limiting factor; China can work with whoever is in power in Myanmar. And if China is flexible, so must other countries be when dealing with China. Indeed, for China, the terms 'open' and 'inclusive' are not only about its willingness to include different countries in its new project but also about creating an openness towards Chinese state-owned enterprises (SOEs) and other agencies involved in the new Silk Roads-related construction. And by constantly underlining the 'win–win' nature and 'common development' objectives of the new Silk Roads, China wishes to consolidate both its diplomatic position and the economic advantages of its enterprises.

However, as the record shows in many countries, once Chinese enterprises have established a presence in a country, Chinese leaders and diplomats are not too far behind in calling for the fair treatment or safety of their enterprises and citizens among other things. This is nothing unusual, of course, and many, if not all, countries do this but this also underlines the problems with China's statements about being a country that does not exercise hegemony or interferes in the internal affairs of other countries. In many respect, while China's articulation and style might differ, it is not very different from the United States in the pursuit of its interests. Especially, given China's fraught political ties in many instances, such as with Vietnam or the Philippines, it is almost inevitable that Chinese enterprises and citizens will be targeted and this can then add to the basket of bilateral problems.[22]

## Conclusion

The foregoing examination of the China–Myanmar relations in the context of the latter's ongoing political transition, and in particular, the impact of the 2015 elections suggests that from China's perspective, there are certainly issues that hold considerable consequence for not just China's external relations but also for its domestic affairs. It also suggests that China has been thinking of 'managing' or dealing with the consequences or spillover of the political changes in Myanmar. No matter the results of Myanmar's elections, China has its broad strategy chalked out which essentially, is one of working with whoever comes to power.

Structural conditions currently are such that China will continue to remain important both politically and economically for Myanmar for some time to come despite the latter's opening up to the rest of the world. In part, this is because the Myanmarese military (*Tatmadaw*) appears unwilling to completely loosen its hold on political affairs of the country, and in part, due to continuing inter-ethnic tensions including the lack of agreement on a federal structure or any similar arrangement that will address the concerns of the ethnic minorities. India has not quite stepped up to the plate as it were—if matching the Chinese influence has been its intent—and thus, the Myanmar government has had also to rely on distant powers or the Association of Southeast Asian Nations to try and offset the Chinese influence. This is not an easy task and will only get harder with a slew of new Chinese diplomatic initiatives in the region.

## NOTES

1. As an aside, it might be added here that the Chinese government also takes very seriously the idea of 'media management'—freedom is not license according to Beijing—and the media serves the public good as defined by the government, not by the public or even by the Constitution.
2. Yun Sun, "China adapts to New Myanmar Reality", *Asia Times Online*, 23 December 2013, http://atimes.com/atimes/Southeast_Asia/SEA-04-231213.html; Xiong Liying, "Zhongguo dui Miandian waijiao zhuanbian de xiao mimi (The secret behind the transformation of China's diplomacy towards Myanmar)", *Ta Kung Pao*, 9 February 2015, http://news.takungpao.com/world/exclusive/2015-02/2916191.html.
3. Keynote Address by Amb. V. Sundararajan Seshadri, *Myanmar: Moving Towards Elections 2015*, Maulana Abul Kalam Azad Institute of Asian Studies, Kolkata, 19 February 2015.
4. Shishir Ghimire, "China and the Federalism Question in Nepal", *ICS Analysis*, No. 11, June 2013, http://www.icsin.org/publications/chin.a-and-the-federalism-question-in-nepal
5. A Chinese company, China Datang Corporation, for instance, paid US$2.4 million to the Kachin Independence Army to resume operation of the Taping hydropower dam and even agreed to divert some power to areas under the control of the rebel group by the terms of the 1994 ceasefire agreement with the Myanmar authorities. Matthew Smith, "How China Fuels Myanmar's Wars", *The New York Times*, 4 March 2015, http://www.nytimes.com/2015/03/05/opinion/how-china-fuels-myanmars-wars.html.
6. Ding Gang, 'Monk Politics a Potential Risk for Myanmar", *Global Times*, 12 April 2013, http://www.globaltimes.cn/content/829850.shtml. See also, Jonathan Head, "Spirit of Defiance at Burma's Monywa Mine", *BBC News*, 30 November 2012, http://www.bbc.com/news/world-asia-20537210
7. See section on "The Chinese Dream", pp.35-70 in Xi Jinping, *The Governance of China* (Beijing: Foreign Languages Press, 2014).

8. Khin Maung Win, "Myanmar's Domestic Issues", Session I: *Myanmar: Moving Towards Elections 2015*, Maulana Abul Kalam Azad Institute of Asian Studies, Kolkata, 19 February 2015.
9. For more on this aspect see Jabin T. Jacob, "India, China and the Coming US Drawdown in Afghanistan: A Choice of Dilemmas", *Economic and Political Weekly*, Vol. XLIX, No. 14, 5 April 2014, pp. 24-27.
10. The work on the dam was first stopped in September 2011. See Rachel Harvey, "Burma Dam: Work Halted on Divisive Myitsone Project", *BBC*, 30 September 2011, http://www.bbc.com/news/world-asia-pacific-15121801 but is now expected to restart in 2015. Mizzima, "Myitsone Dam Project Expected to Resume in 2015, says CPI", 24 January 2013, http://archive-2.mizzima.com/news/inside-burma/8784-myitsone-dam-project-expected-to-resume-in-2015-says-cpi.html
11. *South China Morning Post*, "7 Myanmar Soldiers Killed, 20 Wounded in Rebel Attack near Chinese Border", 16 December 2014, http://www.scmp.com/news/asia/article/1663088/7-myanmar-soldiers-killed-20-wounded-rebel-attack-near-chinese-border
12. Chris Buckley, "Myanmar Warplane Kills Four Farmers in China", *The New York Times*, 13 March, 2015, http://www.nytimes.com/2015/03/14/world/asia/myanmar-warplane-kills-four-farmers-in-china.html?_r=0
13. See for instance, *Sina.com.cn*, "Meidi: Chengdu junqu kongjun budui zuyi baiping Miandian jun ji jia po feiji, (Media: Chengdu Military Region air force troops are sufficient to knock out Myanmar's worn out aircraft)", 16 March 2015, http://mil.news.sina.com.cn/2015-03-16/1136824543.html
14. Yang Danzhi, "Action Needed to Stop Cross-Border Incursions", *China Daily*, 18 March 2015, http://www.chinadaily.com.cn/opinion/2015-03/18/content_19840253.htm; Bai Tiantian, "Myanmar Govt Apologizes for Yunnan Bombing", *Global Times*, 3 April 2015, http://www.globaltimes.cn/content/915229.shtml
15. *The Irrawaddy*, "Second Red Cross Convoy Attacked in Kokang", 22 February 2015, http://www.irrawaddy.org/burma/second-red-cross-convoy-attacked-kokang.html; Bernt Berger, "Is Beijing Supporting Rebel Groups in Myanmar?", *The Interpreter*, 24 February 2015, http://www.lowyinterpreter.org/post/2015/02/24/beijing-support-rebel-groups-myanmar-burma.aspx
16. *Xinhua*, "China to Play Constructive Role in Myanmar Peace Process", 16 February 2015, http://news.xinhuanet.com/english/china/2015-02/16/c_134000949.htm
17. *Xinhua*, "Chinese Vice President Holds Talks with Myanmar Counterpart in Nay Pyi Taw", 17 December 2014, http://news.xinhuanet.com/english/china/2014-12/17/c_133862048.htm
18. *Xinhua*, "Chinese Premier, Myanmar Leaders Vow to Boost Bilateral Ties", 15 November 2014, http://news.xinhuanet.com/english/china/2014-11/15/c_133790825.htm
19. Ministry of External Affairs, Government of India, "Joint Statement on the State Visit of Chinese Premier Li Keqiang to India", *Bilateral/Multilateral Documents*,

20 May 2013, http://www.mea.gov.in/bilateral-documents.htm?dtl/21723/Joint+Statement+on+the+State+Visit+of+Chinese++Li+Keqiang+to+India

20. *Xinhua*, "Chinese Vice President Holds Talks with Myanmar Counterpart in Nay Pyi Taw", 17 December 2014, http://news.xinhuanet.com/english/china/2014-12/17/c_133862048.htm
21. *Xinhua*, "China's "Belt and Road" Initiatives Offer Myanmar New Opportunity: Spokesman", 10 April 2015, http://news.xinhuanet.com/english/2015-04/10/c_134139607.htm; and *Xinhua*, "Myanmar's Ruling Party Voices Support for China's "Belt and Road" Initiative", 8 April 2015, http://news.xinhuanet.com/english/2015-04/08/c_134132439.htm
22. See for example, *Xinhua*, "China Urges Vietnam to Implement Remedies for Riots", 25 August 2014, http://news.xinhuanet.com/english/china/2014-08/25/c_133582938.htm and Mo Jingxi, "Philippines Urged to Protect Chinese Companies", *China Daily*, 26 February 2015, http://www.chinadaily.com.cn/world/2015-02/26/content_19663586.htm

# 8

# Thailand's Policy Towards Myanmar: A Way to Gain International Legitimacy

*Pongkwan Sawasdipakdi*

A national enemy, a devilish country—these notions have played a significant role in the formation of the Thai political memory towards Myanmar, formally known as Burma. Although modern-day diplomatic relations between Thailand and Myanmar only started in 1948, the year then Burma gained its independence, ties between the two ancient kingdoms can be traced back to hundreds of years. With more than 2,000 km of shared border, the Thai–Myanmar relations have been a quagmire of friendship and conflicts. However, the historiography of the Thailand–Myanmar relations, especially from the Thai perspective, focuses mainly on wars and conflicts with little, if any, discussion of positive ties. For instance, the most mentioned events in these land relations are the two Burmese invasions that led to the collapse of Ayutthaya, the old kingdom of Siam, in 1569 and 1767. In fact, the historiography of their relationship was not an accident as the depiction of Thailand's neighbouring countries as enemies had incited a strong sense of nationalism among the Thai people and helped protect the political legitimacy of the elite.[1] Moreover, this nationalism has also provided a justification for the ruling elites to shift Thailand's foreign policy towards Myanmar from cooperative to confrontational.

Although it may seem that Thailand's relations with Myanmar have been predominantly defined by tension, they have, in fact, fluctuated between the periods of conflict and cooperation. The available literature on their bilateral relations has been dominated by narrative works describing the changes in Thailand's foreign policy towards Myanmar without any explanation or reason. Apart from these narrative works, literature that is set to analyse the Thai foreign policy initiatives usually adopts an analytical approach—an overarching framework that concurrently analyses the international and national factors to assess a country's foreign policy. This can be seen from the work of Innes-Brown and Valencia, as they try to explain Thailand's changing resource diplomacy in Indochina and Myanmar. Innes-Brown and Valencia argue that despite the constraints imposed by international-level elements, national-level factors still play a major role.[2] On the other hand, Pavin Chachavalpongpun focuses more on the domestic factors arguing that the fluctuations in Thai–Myanmar relationship have been due to a combination of structural reasons and the role of the Thai elites. He adds that the conduct of foreign policy is complicated by the involvement of multiple actors who compete to protect their own interests.[3]

This paper combines these two approaches. It argues that the international-level element such as the pressure imposed by the Western powers reached its highest point during the Cold War. As a result, the Thai ruling elites decided to bandwagon with the United States, siding with the "Free World". Ergo, Thailand curtailed diplomatic relations with Myanmar at the height of the Cold War. However towards the end of the Cold War external pressure on Thailand's foreign policy towards Myanmar gradually declined and became limited. On the contrary, it was rather dependent on the policy priority of each subsequent Thai government. Even though the West imposed sanctions on Myanmar in response to the military crackdown on student rallies in August 1988 and the arrest of Aung San Suu Kyi, Thailand decided to pursue a cooperative trade policy with Myanmar.

Some might argue that the domestic factors influencing the fluctuations of Thailand's foreign policy towards Myanmar involve the characteristics of different regime types: the military government might be more hostile towards Myanmar than the civilian ones. However, this has been proven wrong. The civilian government of Chuan Leekpai, for example, adopted the Western countries' stance, consistently commenting on Myanmar's state of human rights and democracy. This hindered improvements in Thai–Myanmar relations. The fluctuations in Thailand's policy towards Myanmar since the end of the Cold War can be better traced to the interests of the contesting groups and individuals involved in the policy process.

Moreover, a number of individuals have repeatedly shaped the Thai policy direction towards Myanmar.

This paper is divided into two sections. The first part covers the evolution of Thailand–Myanmar bilateral relations from 1948 until 2014—the year of the most recent military coup d'état in Thailand. The second section covers the Thailand–Myanmar bilateral relationship since the 2014 Thai coup. It will also investigate the obstacles and opportunities posed by the recent regime change in Thailand.

## The Fluctuations of Thailand's Policy towards Myanmar

The fluctuations of Thailand's foreign policy towards Myanmar can be categorised into four periods. The first period began with Myanmar's independence from Great Britain in 1948 and ended with Ne Win's coup against the democratic government in 1962. This period marked a new era in Thai-Myanmar relations since all the prior interactions had been between the Thai government and the British colonial government. The second period spanned from 1962 to 1986. This period saw a significant deterioration in Thailand–Myanmar relationship due to the politics of the Cold War. The third period began with the restoration of the Thailand–Myanmar relations in 1986 to 2010. In this period, Thailand and Myanmar ties were the most inconsistent, starting off with the normalisation of relations but encountering a number of hiccups. The last period was characterised by Myanmar's embarking on political and economic reforms. Following a surge of diplomatic engagement from the Western countries with Myanmar, Thailand, without hesitation, resumed its cooperative stance with the country.

## 1948–1962: Restoring Bilateral Relations

As mentioned earlier, modern-day bilateral relations between Thailand and Myanmar only started in 1948 when Myanmar declared its independence from Great Britain. This does not, however, imply that the two countries lacked contact prior to 1948. Rather, the relationship between the two countries had already existed for hundreds of years, but early bilateral relations were not restricted to the modern concept of statehood—especially the concept of a settled boundary. Although Thailand and Myanmar concluded demarcation of their boundaries in 1825, prior to 1948, Thailand had established diplomatic relations with Myanmar, not through interactions with the Myanmarese government, but with the British colonial government. There was not much cooperation or conflict. Rather, the interactions between the two neighbours prior to 1948 were dominated by the fear that Thailand might also be colonised.

After Myanmar gained independence, Thailand–Myanmar relations remained rocky. Mutual distrust dominated the bilateral relations for almost ten years after 1948. Suspicions intensified when the Kuomintang (KMT), defeated by the Chinese Communist Party in 1949, retreated southwards and took the area along Thailand–Myanmar border as its stronghold. The KMT armies gradually gained control over the area of the Shan State and undermined the central Myanmarese government's authority in the region. The Myanmarese government believed that the Thai government was covertly supporting the KMT, leading to the deterioration of bilateral relations.[4] In 1955, the Thailand–Myanmar relations saw a sign of improvement. U Nu, the then Prime Minister of Myanmar, paid his first official visit to Thailand, in an attempt to fix the bad blood between the two countries. Apart from Thailand, U Nu also embarked on a world trip aimed at establishing diplomatic relations with countries like the United States of America, Japan and Russia. Following U Nu's visit to Thailand, the Prime Minister of Thailand, Field Marshall Phibun and their Majesties, the King and the Queen, reciprocated visits to Myanmar. These events tightened ties between the two, resulting in a growing number of high level visits between the officials of the two countries. The pleasant bilateral relations did not last for long. A coup against U Nu led by General Ne Win immediately interrupted bilateral cooperation and led to the gradual deterioration of friendly exchanges between them.[5]

## 1962–1986: Defending Thailand from the Communist Threat

As soon as U Nu was deposed, General Ne Win proclaimed the "Burmese Way to Socialism" policy and closed Myanmar to the rest of the world. While Myanmar affiliated itself with socialism, Thailand overtly sided with the Western countries with anti-communist sentiments. Anti-communism became the main element of Thailand's foreign policy towards the neighbouring countries and Myanmar was not an exception.[6] Bilateral contacts including top-level dialogue almost halted.[7] Mutual distrust between the two countries led to armed clashes between the Thai and Myanmarese army. To defend itself from a perceived Myanmarese communist threat, Thailand established the "buffer state" policy, supplying weapons to anti-communist ethnic minorities along the Thailand–Myanmar border. This intensified the level of mutual mistrust and severed bilateral relations.

Although official bilateral relations crumbled, ties between the leading Thai and Myanmarese military elites flourished for most of the 1970s and 1980s. This was because Myanmar became increasingly isolationist; its economy fell into a state of despair. With abundant natural resources, Myanmar quickly became Thailand's source for gems, teak and marine products. A number of military elite were involved in stitching ties with the Myanmar government. These elite included, but were not limited to, Generals Kriangsak Chomanand, Prem Tinsulanonda and Chaovalit Yongchaiyudh.[8] These names would repeatedly reappear in the subsequent periods of the Thailand–Myanmar relations, demonstrating the importance of individual friendship in Thailand's policy process. In fact, despite implementation of the buffer state policy, ties between the Thai and Myanmarese armies existed. However, the military-to-military ties had to be hidden from the Cold War environment that did not allow Thailand to overtly pursue cooperation with Myanmar. Thailand's policy towards Myanmar started to shift in the late 1980s, and continued thus till the end of the Cold War. Corporations became the domain of Thailand–Myanmar bilateral relations in the subsequent period.

## 1986–2010: A Period of Policy Turbulences

In the late 1980s, weakening Cold War tensions allowed Thailand to pursue cooperative relations with Myanmar, despite Myanmar remaining a military-controlled socialist country. At the same time, Myanmar's destitute economy forced the country to open up, at least, to border trade with Thailand. However as mentioned earlier, despite limited political interaction and relations, the military-to-military ties had been successfully established. With decreasing tension in international politics, the then prime minister of Thailand, General Prem Tinsulanonda, imposed the "omni-directional policy", aiming to improve bilateral relations with the neighbouring countries. A series of official visits by Thai officials to Myanmar began in 1986, starting with the Foreign Minister ACM Siddhi Savetsila, Princess Sirindhorn and the Thai Army Chief Chavalit Yonchaiyudh. These visits resulted in tightening relations between the two countries. In addition, the two countries also agreed to revive the Joint Border Committee, a mechanism established to deal with the prolonged border disputes.[9]

However, major changes did not occur until General Chatichai Choonhavan assumed premiership in 1988. One of Chatichai's policy initiatives was to "turn battlefields into marketplaces" "aiming to restore the relations with Indochina that crumbled in previous years due to the Cold War". As for Myanmar, Chatichai announced "Constructive Engagement" that would accommodate Myanmar with regional realities.[10] Consequently, Thailand, together with Singapore, cooperatively supported the Association of Southeast Asian Nations (ASEAN) initiatives to engage

Myanmar.[11] Undoubtedly, economic benefits were on top of the agenda under Chatichai's premiership. Other than proactive economic cooperation with Myanmar, army-to-army relations also played an important role in extracting concessions from Myanmar for the Thai companies to extract natural resources.[12] The direct investment of Thai business inside Myanmar grew in numbers.

The accommodative foreign policy towards Myanmar ended with the overthrow of the Chatichai government in 1991 in a coup d'état. The coup's goal was to address the domestic issues including corruption and abuse of power. Consequently, the military government adopted a more inward-looking policy while foreign policy lost its priority. Following two unsuccessful years under the military government, Thailand returned to democratic rule under the Democrat Party after the elections in 1993. However, with the return of a civilian government in power, it hardened Thailand's foreign policy towards Myanmar's military junta. Thailand's Myanmar policy shifted again when the following election brought Banharn Silpa-archa to power in 1995 and General Chavalit in 1996. Under the premiership of General Chavalit who played a significant role in improving ties between the Thai and Myanmarese armies in the 1970s and 1980s, Thailand reimposed an engagement policy towards Myanmar. Thailand even supported Myanmar to join ASEAN in 1997. This was claimed to be a policy of pulling Myanmar out of China's sphere of influence.[13]

But the engagement policy was short-lived as the democratic government returned to power in 1997 in Thailand. Surin Phitsuwan, the then Thai Foreign Minister and later ASEAN's Secretary, was particularly vocal about Myanmar's democracy and human rights situation. In addition, two incidents severely hampered the Thailand–Myanmar relations in 1999–2000. The first event involved a student dissident group taking over the Myanmarese embassy in Bangkok in 1999. The Thai government handled the situation lightly, which infuriated the Myanmarese government. As a result, the Myanmar government sealed all the border crossings. The other incident involved a group of armed Karen insurgents storming a hospital in a province of Thailand. Although the Thai government was able to resolve both the incidents quickly, they dragged the bilateral relations to one of lowest, if not to the lowest point in modern history.[14]

Thailand's foreign policy towards Myanmar shifted again after Thaksin Shinawatra won the 2001 elections. This was considered to be the peak of Thai–Myanmar bilateral relations. His "constructive engagement" policy was based on economic interests and in accommodating Myanmar's preferences. Apart from economic interests that had benefitted Chatichai's government, many recurrent actors, including General Chavalit, played significant roles in the Thaksin government. Figure 1 depicts the total bilateral trade, export and import values, and the balance of trade between Thailand and Myanmar from 2000 to 2008. The Figure shows that since Thaksin was elected in 2001, bilateral trade between Thailand and Myanmar significantly increased, especially after 2005 when Thaksin won his second landslide election, boosting his confidence in veering his policy of more aggressively engaging Myanmar.

One of the reasons behind a slower growth in bilateral trade in 2001–2003 was Myanmar's reluctance to accept Thailand's political incentives and diplomatic initiatives aimed at encouraging domestic reform in Myanmar. In 2003, Thaksin's administration initiated the "Bangkok Process", which would allow external monitoring of Myanmar's internal affairs. Of course, the initiative was unacceptable to Myanmar's junta, causing it to withdraw its participation. However, the fragility of Myanmar's economy eventually forced the junta to promote trade relations with Thailand. The total bilateral trade climbed from approximately $1.3 billion in 2003 to approximately $2 billion and $2.5 billion in 2004 and 2005, respectively.

**Figure 1: Total Bilateral Trade, Export and Import Values and Trade Balance between Thailand and Myanmar, 2000–2008.**

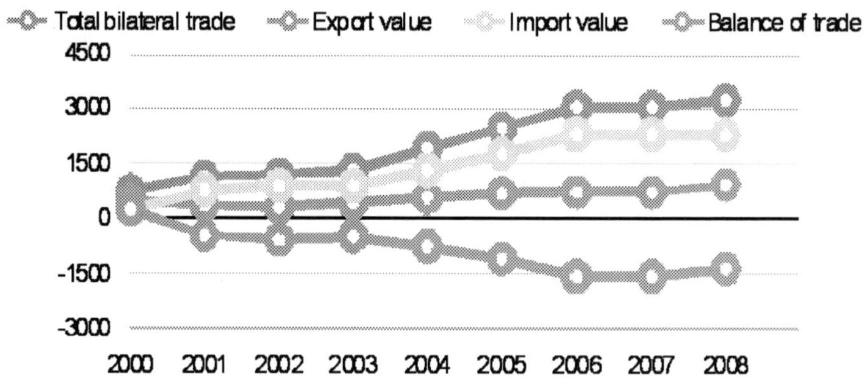


*Source:* Thailand Ministry of Commerce.

In 2006, the Thai military ousted Thaksin from power, causing a slight change in the Thailand–Myanmar relations. Unlike Thaksin's administration, the coup-appointed government did not have a specific policy towards Myanmar.[15] In 2007, Myanmar faced another wave of strong condemnation by foreign countries as a result of the military crackdown of protesters in the so-called "Saffron Revolution". Nevertheless, Thailand's foreign policy under the premiership of Samak Sundaravej, who rose to power in 2008, was clear: Thailand would oppose the sanctions imposed by the Western countries against Myanmar and it would re-establish the economic ties with the country.[16] Thailand was arguably the only country that the Myanmarese government could trust and was allowed to enter Myanmar to provide humanitarian aid for victims of Cyclone Nargis. Thailand was called Myanmar's spokesperson at the international level.[17] However, there a major political shift following contestations in Thailand leading to another change in government and foreign policy towards Myanmar. Abhisit Vejjajive, the Democrat Party's new leader, was elected in 2008. Abhisit re-imposed the Democratic-styled tough stance towards Myanmar. During his visit to Naypyidaw, Abhisit revisited the rhetoric of democratisation and modernisation to his Myanmar counterparts. This policy direction continued until Myanmar underwent political and economic transformations in 2010.

The fluctuations of the Thai foreign policy towards Myanmar raised a number of questions regarding the factors causing these changes. The international-level element including the policy stance of the West towards Myanmar did not appear to have consistent effect on Thailand's policy. While the Western stance towards Myanmar remained essentially stable, except for the crackdown in 2007 when the West increased its condemnation of the Myanmar junta, the effects on Thailand's policy varied. These foreign policy inconsistencies can be explained through domestic-level analysis. There are at least two concepts that can be applied: competing interests and legitimacy. First and foremost, competing interest groups have played important roles in shaping Thailand's policy towards Myanmar. Apart from sharing the same policy advisors, business interests had been the main driver of Thailand's foreign policies during the Chatichai, Thaksin and other pro-Thaksin governments. In contrast, the policy direction of the Democrat governments was set by a particular group of persons who tended to adopt Western norms. The second domestic factor, which is closely related to competing interests, is that the two camps employed two different concepts of legitimacy. Apart from being democratically elected, for Chatichai's and Thaksin's government, they believed that economic development grants domestic and international legitimacy. As a result, with the main focus on business interests, they could consolidate its legitimacy without following the Western stance on international issues. In contrast, the Democrat Party tended to uphold its legitimacy by gaining international acceptance. Especially Abisit's government, which was brought to power after the constitutional court had dissolved the Phue Thai Party—the previous ruling party—tried to regain international acceptance by reversing the existing cooperative policy with Myanmar.

## 2010–Present: Policy towards Transitional Myanmar

Myanmar's political and economic reforms since 2010 have influenced the Thailand–Myanmar relations. Myanmar has gradually become more open and has welcomed foreign direct investments, aid and accommodative policies from foreign countries. With the Myanmarese government's firm determination for reform, foreign countries, especially those of the West, have been more attentive to Myanmar's development and have welcomed the new sign of changes by gradually removing sanctions and being more cooperative with Myanmar.

Myanmar conducted its first election after several decades of military rule in 2011. At the same time, Thailand's election brought Yingluck Shinawatra, the sister of the ousted Prime Minister Thaksin Shinawatra, to power. Yingluck restored an accommodative policy towards Myanmar originally enacted by the Thaksin supporters, but this time with an absolute green light from the West. Again, Thailand's policy towards Myanmar under the Yingluck government was based on economic interests. During her first visit to Myanmar in 2011, Yingluck assured that Thailand would not allow any armed group to use its soil as a base to launch attacks against the Myanmarese army. Both countries also agreed to further their existing cooperation and explore new development opportunities. These agreements included Myanmar's assurance to reopen the border checkpoint at Maesot, closed since 2010 as a protest against the construction of a slope bank protection on the Mei River. Thailand has also agreed to support infrastructure development in Myanmar including road construction, road improvement and development of the Dawei special economic zone.[18]

Among the accommodative policies towards Myanmar, the two priorities of Yingluck government are to successfully develop the Dawei Project and to establish special economic zones in districts along the borders with the neighbouring countries. In 2010, the Italian–Thai Development (ITD), a Thai private company, was awarded a contract by the Myanmarese government to develop the Dawei Project. However, ITD was unable to accumulate sufficient capital to develop the project within the set time frame. In 2012, the Thai government decided to take over the project and ITD was changed into one of the many stakeholders.[19] The Dawei Project represents significant economic opportunities for Thailand and Myanmar. Not only does it include a deep seaport, but also includes facilities such as an airport, roads and railroads connecting Thailand and Myanmar and industrial parks. The Dawei deep seaport will be significantly beneficial to ASEAN's economic development since it is a gateway to the west.[20] Currently, the crowded Malacca Straits is the only connector to the Indian Ocean. The Dawei deep seaport can reduce the traffic in the Straits and decrease costs and time for the producers and exporters exporting goods from Southeast Asia to the western regions. Although the Thai government has backed the project, Yingluck's government has had a hard time attracting investors in this area.

Another plan to improve the border trade with the neighbouring countries under the Yingluck government has been aimed to establish special economic zones in the border cities with a high economic growth potential. The Mae Sot district in the Tak province was the chosen city on the Thailand–Myanmar border. Together with the development of a special economic zone on the Thai side, Myanmar also planned to establish Myawaddy as a "twin city"—a special economic zone on the Myanmar border. The special economic zones will provide special treatments for investors as well as support for the use of labour and resources from the neighbouring countries.[21] The Thai government has also planned to develop highways and railroads connecting the two cities as this would reduce the travelling time for both visitors and investors to these two areas.[22]

## The Development of the Thailand–Myanmar Relations after Thailand's 2014 Coup

The Thai army staged a military coup against the Yingluck government in 2014 and ousted her from power. Although the military government carried out its old good-neighbourly behaviour towards Myanmar as under Yingluck's government, the sense of nationalism went amiss, affecting the bilateral relations. General Prayuth Chan-Ocha, the Prime Minister and the coup leader, chose Myanmar as the first destination of his introductory visit. During his visit, General Prayuth signed three MoUs with Myanmar to establish twin cities in three areas.[23] The priorities of Thailand's policy direction towards Myanmar under the premiership of General Prayuth focuses on three areas: 1) to complete the establishment of the special economic zones; 2) to continue the construction of the Dawei Project and 3) to systemise the registration of migrant workers. While there is a strong political will on both sides to meet their shared commitments, the ability to expedite these efforts is questionable.[24]

Prayuth's government has been very active in opening up the special economic zones. He has set 2016 as the year for the completion of the Special Economic Zones between the two neighbours. This phase will cover five areas, including the Mae Sai district that will pair up with Thachileik in Myanmar.[25] Despite the conflicting views on SEZs across different sectors, these zones will provide Thailand with great economic opportunities. First, the SEZs will attract a number of investors seeking better investment conditions. Second, it will allow higher trade activities between the two neighbours because of free trade rules. Third, there is a large possibility that in the future Thailand will take advantage of Myanmar's privilege of GSP with Europe, the United States and Japan. This will advance the export opportunities for Thailand.[26]

In addition to the development of SEZs, Prayuth's government has been committed to accelerate the Dawei Project. This project, if on track, will be completed by 2025.[27] Moreover, the present military government also emphasises on the need to register the migrant workers, including those from Myanmar. The registration process is complicated by the fact that these migrant workers are required to provide their proof of citizenship. This process cannot be fulfilled without assistance from their countries of origin.[28] Again, there is a strong political will from both Thailand and Myanmar to cooperate in these issues, but any progress will rely on the capabilities of both the sides.

However, these economic opportunities are not without challenges. Certainly, numerous persisting cross-border problems such as drug-trafficking, human trafficking and illegal trade pose significant challenges to Thailand. The major frustrations arising under the military government are its world-security view and the negative perception of Myanmar that potentially obstruct cooperation. For example, on the issue of the SEZ, the government believes that while such zones will attract more investors, they would also act as a barrier preventing the migrant workers to migrate into the "inner zones" of the country. This is because the military believes that the influx of migrant workers to other parts of the country will result in increase in criminal activities and other related problems.[29] Another example demonstrating the return of nationalism was when General Prayuth claimed that the person who had killed two Western tourists in southern Thailand was a Myanmarese migrant worker. Of course, the claim lacked sufficient evidence and resulted in a response from Thein Sein,

Myanmar's President. Fortunately, economic interests of both the countries are intricately intertwined and the conflict did turn into a significant issue.

Adding to the numerous challenges is the Rohingya problem. Because of the political tensions and violence in Myanmar, a number of Rohingyas sailed across the Indian Ocean and some of their boats got stranded in Thailand. Instead of following the humanitarian aid standards, the Thai navy decided to push these migrants out of Thailand's border. Although the legality of the Navy's practice towards the Rohingyas is debatable, public opinion normally equates such humanitarian assistance with anti-nationalism. Though the link between these two issues are not clear, it has become part of a recent social discourse.

## Conclusion

Overall, the Thailand–Myanmar bilateral relations have been characterised by rapid fluctuations and inconsistencies. There are several factors affecting the policy changes, which can be divided into domestic-level and international-level elements. Certainly, these two types of elements yield asymmetric pressures on the policymaking of Thailand's foreign policy towards Myanmar. As mentioned earlier, differences in the policy priority of each government has created a discontinuity in the Thai foreign policy towards Myanmar. Thanks to the existing negative public perception of Myanmar, the Thai government has little trouble reversing policies that had led to improved Thai–Myanmar relations. Since 2010, the trend of Thailand's foreign policy towards Myanmar has taken a positive trajectory. Although the negative perception of Myanmar by the Thai general public and the political elite still appears to be problematic, the embedded interests of multidimensional economic cooperation prevent complete interruption of bilateral relations. Therefore, it can be assumed that despite possible differences in the minor details of Thailand's foreign policy towards Myanmar under each government, a complete reversal of the policy trajectory is almost unexpected in the near future.

### NOTES

1. Pavin Chachavalpongpun, "Thailand-Myanmar Relations: Old Animosity in a New Bilateral Setting", *International Relations in Southeast Asia: Between Bilateralism and* Multilateralism, ed. N. Genevan and Ramses Amer (Singapore: Institute of Southeast Asian Studies, 2010) 117-118.
2. Marc Innes-Brown and Mark J. Valencia, "Thailand's Resource Diplomacy in Indochina and Myanmar", *Contemporary Southeast Asia* 14.4 (March 1993): 341-344.
3. Chachavalpongpun, 124-125.

4. Kavi Chongkittavon,"Thai-Burma Relations", *Challenges to Democratization in Burma*, ed. International Institute for Democracy and Electoral Assistance (Stockholm, International Institute for Democracy and Electoral Assistance) 117-118.
5. Chongkittavon, 119.
6. Chachavalpongpun 118-119.
7. Chongkittavon, 119.
8. N. Genevan, 138.
9. Chongkittavon, 119-120.
10. Chachavalpongpun, 121.
11. N. Genesan, "Thai-Myanmar-ASEAN Relations: The Politics of Face and Grace,"*Asian Affairs: An American Review* 33.3 (2006): 138.
12. Innes-Brown and Mark J. Valencia, 332-351.
13. Chachavalpongpun, 122.
14. Genevan, 139-140.
15. Chachavalpongpun, 124.
16. Chachavalpongpun, 125.
17. "Paed Pee Kwam Sampan Thai-Burma Kwam Kudyaeng Lae Pol Pra Yot [8 Years of Thai-Myanmar Relationship: Conflicts and Interests] *Salween News*, 28 June 2011, online, Internet, 30 Apr. 2015. Available: http://salweennews.org/home/?p=267.
18. "Thailand, Myanmar Agree to Strengthen Cooperation at all Levels", *Royal Thai Embassy Singapore*, online, Internet. 30 April, 2015. Available at: http://www.thaiembassy.sg/press_media/news-highlights/thailand-myanmar-agree-to-strengthen-cooperation-at-all-levels.
19. "Kia Italian-Thai Phon Tawai Project Yok Het Khad Ngern Wain Kuen Tee Din 250 Lan Doll Ratthaban Thai-Burma Cho Send Sampathan Chabab Mai" [Removed Italian-Thai from the Dawei Project for Being Short for 250 Million Dollar for Expropriating Lands, The Thai-Myanmar Governments Lined up for a New Contract] *Thai Republica.* 23 Jan, 2013, online, Internet, 30 April 2015. Available at: http://thaipublica.org/2013/01/reject-italianthai-dawei-project/.
20. "Thein Sein Choon Ratthaban Yingluck Game Rue Yai Tawai Project" [Thein Sein Not Satisfied with Yingluck's Government Handling with the Dawei Project] *Thai Republica*, online, Internet. 30 April 2015. Available: http://thaipublica.org/2012/06/thein-sein-yingluck/.
21. "Yingluck Prachoom Khet Settakit Piset Kamnod Suksa 5 Phak" [Yingluck Set up Meeting about the Special Economic Zones in 5 Regions] *Manager*, 16 September 2013, online, Internet. 30 Apr. 2015. Available: http://www.manager.co.th/Politics/ViewNews.aspx?NewsID=9560000118007.
22. "Poo Long Chai Daen Mae Sot Tam Kueb Na Khed Settakit Piset" [Yingluck Visited the Border City Mae Sot to Follow the Development of the Special Economic Zone Project]
23. Prayuth Yuen Burma 9-10 Tulakhom Send MOU 3 Chabab [Prayuth Visiting Myanmar on October 9-10, Signing Three MOUs] Bangkok Biz News, 8 October 2014, online, Internet. 30 Apr. 2015. Available at: http://www.bangkokbiznews.com/news/detail/609878.

24. Interview with a Thai diplomate overseeing Thailand–Myanmar relations, 8 February 2015.
25. "Dun Setthakit Piset Phase 2 Fai Kieu Noon Tung Eek 5 Jungwad Took Pak Sung Sapapat Tum Pan RermPattana" [Pushing the Second Phase of Special Economic Zones in 5 Provinces, Asking NESBD to Start the Development Plan] *Thai Chamber of Commerce,* online, Internet, 30 April 2015. Available: http://www.thaichamber.org/scripts/detail.asp?nNEWSID=12129.
26. Anon Tantiwiwat, "Khet Settakit Piset Tai Ngao Kor Sor Chor Kwam Laklan Khong Jot Kan Pattana Settakid Bon Than Kwam Kid KwamMankong" [Special Economic Zones under NCPO, the Overlapping Ideas of Economic Development and Security] *Bio Thai.* 22Aug. 2014, online, Internet, 30 April 2015. Available at: http://www.biothai.net/news/23333.
27. Sasithorn Ongdee, "Dawei Construction Could Be Back on Track Soon", *The Nation*, 5 Jan. 2015. online, Internet. 30 Apr. 2015. Available at: http://www.nationmultimedia.com/business/Dawei-construction-could-be-back-on-track-soon-30251184.html
28. "Rattamontree Raengngan Reng Chat Rabiab Raengngan Tang Dao Lung Sin Sood 31 Meenakhom Nee" [Labor Minister Looks to Regulate Migrant Workers after the Process Finished on March 31. *National News Bureau of Thailand,* 24 March 2015, online, Internet, 30 April 2015. Available at: http://thainews.prd.go.th/centerweb/News/NewsDetail?NT01_NewsID=WNSOC5803240010083.
29. Tantiwiwat.

# 9

# Bangladesh's Relations with a Changing Myanmar: Determinants, Dynamics, Constraints and Promises

*Ehsanul Haque*

## Introduction

Bangladesh sustains an enduring, substantive and promising bilateral relationship with Myanmar. The relationship is officially described as "good neighbourly", "friendly", "cooperative" and "reciprocal". Indeed, the two neighbouring countries share a long-standing bond underpinned by historical, cultural, commercial and social ties. Today, the relationship qualifies as cordial and reciprocal, and it has progressively been broadened and raised to a mature level. While this is not an exaggeration of the current state of the Bangladesh–Myanmar bilateral relations, Bangladesh evidently realises the necessity of cultivating Myanmar more in its foreign policy priorities. For its part, Myanmar considers Bangladesh an increasingly important neighbour too.

Myanmar is the second largest of Bangladesh's immediate neighbour after India. It is one of the key players in the Bay of Bengal littoral region and shares land and maritime boundaries with Bangladesh.[1] Myanmar's importance to Bangladesh derives, in part, from its geographical location given that it is Myanmar where South Asia, Southeast Asia and the northern part of East Asia intersect. The geographic proximity between the two countries provides an opportunity for building a more productive, broad-based, stable and peaceful bilateral relationship. In fact, Myanmar is strategically important to Bangladesh as the latter's "gateway" to China and the countries in Southeast Asia, and from an economic standpoint, as a potential long-term supplier of natural gas.[2] Moreover, Myanmar's territorial size, natural resources, vast pool of low-cost labour and educated class offer greater prospects of development than is the case in Southeast Asia's other countries. In addition, Myanmar is poised to become the nexus of new road, rail, and shipping links that can foster connectivity between Bangladesh and East and Southeast Asia.[3]

Conversely, Bangladesh matters to Myanmar on politico-strategic and economic grounds. The growing importance of Bangladesh in Myanmar's foreign policy calculations can be attributed to a number of factors and conditions, one of which is Bangladesh's geographic location as Myanmar's gateway to the eastern part of India and other South Asian countries including Nepal and Bhutan.[4] Indeed, certain geostrategic developments and escalating economic and security challenges in South Asia and the Asia-Pacific region have accorded Bangladesh a degree of importance to Myanmar. Hence, Bangladesh's relation with Myanmar must be placed in its broader geopolitical and geoeconomic settings.

Myanmar was one of the earliest countries to recognise the sovereignty and independence of Bangladesh on January 13, 1972.[5] On March 21, 1972, the two countries officially established diplomatic relations at the ambassadorial level,[6] and the relationship began on a cordial footing. One of the significant indications of the improvement in bilateral relations between Bangladesh and Myanmar has been a series of high-level visits by the heads of states and officials from the two countries. Most of these visits have been marked by signing of broad agreements on increased bilateral cooperation in multifarious fields. A high point in the bilateral relationship came with the visit by the Bangladeshi Prime Minister Sheikh Hasina to Myanmar in 2011.

Over the years, elements of cooperation and competition have characterised the bilateral ties without seriously undermining the broad contours of the relationship. Today, relations between Bangladesh and Myanmar are facing new realities and pressures in view of the political and economic reforms introduced in 2011 by the new/reformist government of Myanmar. Arguably, the recent relationship between the two countries has been determined by this transformation and shift in Myanmar's domestic politics.

The reform process in Myanmar appears to have been viewed in Bangladesh with a sense of optimism and belief that tremendous opportunity lie ahead for a more political engagement and greater economic cooperation and development, which would help overcome difficulties between the two countries. Obviously, on key foreign policy issues like the relationship with Myanmar, different regimes and power elites in Bangladesh have been successful in articulating a unified and coherent position.

## Political Transition/Economic Reforms and a Changing Myanmar

Myanmar is currently at a defining moment in its history—it is in the midst of a far-reaching transformation that has heralded a new beginning for the country. After decades of military dictatorship, long international isolation and economic stagnation, the country has returned to a constitutional and parliamentary rule. The present civilian government of Myanmar led by moderate, persuasive and reformist President Thein Sein unleashed a wave of political and economic reforms in 2011. As a result, Myanmar is witnessing gradual reforms from authoritarianism to the inauguration of greater political and economic openness. With the national elections scheduled for late 2015 and also with the prospect of a democratically elected government's assumption of power, the leaders of the country are committed to build a new and different Myanmar—one that is democratic, inclusive , peaceful with a sustainable economic growth and development.

This section examines the domestic context in which Myanmar's policy towards the external world has been formulated and explores how Myanmar's foreign policy has been embedded within its broader policy responses. If one looks at the drivers of Myanmar's external relations largely from a domestic perspective, it would be clear that Myanmar's foreign policy has inextricably been intertwined with the country's underlying domestic conditions and considerations.

In line with the 2011 reform agenda, Myanmar legalised political protests and trade unions; liberalised media; lifted/eased Internet restrictions; instituted currency reforms; granted amnesty to and released most political prisoners; abolished a twenty-five year ban on public gatherings and incorporated a few civil society groups including former political opponents into the governmental advisory bodies.[7] Moreover, Myanmar has effectively begun a reconciliation process with the country's ethnic minorities by concluding ceasefires to end ethnic civil wars and has also negotiated with the democratic oppositions which has signalled that the country is on the road to democracy and pluralism. In addition,

Myanmar has achieved extraordinary democratic gains by conducting relatively free and competitive parliamentary by-elections in 2012 in which the opposition National League for Democracy (NLD) had joined the mainstream politics by winning 43 out of the 44 seats it had contested, enabling the pro-democracy icon Aung San Suu Kyi to enter Parliament and assume key role in various legislative committees, including the one set up to revise the country's Constitution.[8]

In the changing political environment, Myanmar's four main stakeholders—political parties, ethnic groups, the *Tatmadaw* (military) and the *Sangha* (the Buddhist monastic community)—have a historic opportunity to play a role in shaping its future.[9] The momentous developments brought by the reform process have allowed Thein Sein room to negotiate, bargain and seek compromise between Myanmar's conflicting perspectives with the West. In response to such reform drives, the international community decided to ease the economic sanctions imposed on them earlier. Once considered the "Rice Bowl of Asia", Myanmar is rising once again as democratic reforms championed by Thein Sein continue to progress and industries like energy, telecommunication and agriculture enjoy the benefits of foreign investment and trade liberalisation. It is clear that currently investor optimism in Myanmar runs very high and the flow/volume of Foreign Direct Investment (FDI) in the country has seen a conspicuous rise. Although the FDI as of 2011 stood at $ 2 billion, rising to $2.7 billion in 2013, the investment is expected to accelerate more in future.[10] Meanwhile, the reformist government has, to a great deal, invested in infrastructure projects for capacity building, earmarking special economic zones for foreign-funded industrial complexes.[11] In addition, the Asian Development Bank (ADB) resumed loans to Myanmar in 2013 for the first time in thirty years with the aim to boost its socio-economic sector. Now, the new Myanmar leadership can claim to have achieved substantial success in improving its relations with the West since the reform programme was launched in 2011.

Myanmar carries a considerable economic weight in the region as its economic targets include augmenting the annual Gross Domestic Product (GDP) growth rates as high as 8.8 percent for the projected future and in tripling the GDP per capita by 2016 and in reducing poverty from 26 percent to 16 percent.[12] These steps are geared towards achieving the country's target of being the region's first "lion economy".[13] A recent study by the ADB reveals that the country is capable of achieving an annual economic growth of as much as 8 percent and more than tripling its per capita income of $ 3,000 by 2030 if it succeeds in continuing its current reform trajectory. Myanmar is poised to become one of the next rising stars in Asia if it can successfully leverage its rich endowments—natural resources, labour force and geographic advantage—for economic development and growth.[14] From 1988–2010, Myanmar's GDP rose from $ 12.6 billion to $ 45.4 billion, while imports increased from $ 246 million to $ 4.8 billion; exports rose from $ 167 million to $ 8.7 billion and foreign investment from $ 4 million to $ 8.3 billion.[15] Unsurprisingly, sweeping reforms in Myanmar's political and economic landscape have generated huge interest in multiple sectors of the economy including oil and gas, mining, power, industrial estate development, manufacturing and the like. In fact, Myanmar has untapped markets and unexploited natural resources including substantial reserves of minerals, petroleum and timber.[16] The leaders of the country now appear more committed to the creation of a stable, unified, peaceful, democratic and prosperous Myanmar.

The scope and pace of Myanmar's ongoing democratic reforms significantly influences the conduct of the country's foreign relations. One of the major thrusts of Myanmar's current foreign policy has been to secure recognition from the international community as the region's potential power. To be sure, Myanmar actively seeks to diversify its foreign policy, exploit its geopolitical potential, play a regional leadership role and gain more room for maneuvering in the global community. After the reform drive was announced and the economic and business interests set the tone for Myanmar's foreign relations, geopolitical and geoeconomic considerations began to feature prominently in Myanmar's foreign policy.

For long, the main arena for Myanmar's international relations had remained confined to its relationship with the Association of Southeast Asian Nations (ASEAN) and its multilateral and bilateral relations with its fellow ASEAN members.[17] However, the country's new foreign policy activism is particularly evident in its successful completion of the ASEAN chairmanship for 2014[18] which reflected the country's interest and capacity to interact not only with the region but also with the external world from a position of power and responsibility. Indeed, its leadership role in the ASEAN bolstered its political legitimacy, international status, domestic pride and boosted the government's domestic popularity. In recent years, Myanmar has launched a number of new foreign policy initiatives that have elevated the country's international stature and regional influence. The country succeeded in pushing up its weight in international affairs when it successfully hosted several high-profile international events including the 25$^{th}$ ASEAN Summit and the 9$^{th}$ East Asia Summit in November 2014, the 3$^{rd}$ Bay of Bengal Initiative for Multi-Sectoral Technical and Economic Cooperation (BIMSTEC) Summit in March 2014, the 22nd World Economic Forum on East Asia (WEF-EA)[19] in June 2013, and the 27th Southeast Asian Games in December 2013.

Myanmar's current foreign policy focuses on a vision of "Look West policy", designed to build its friendship with the West and Asian countries, and most importantly, to balance China's influence in Myanmar.[20] In fact, Myanmar was used to be perceived by many as one of China's three close allies along with North Korea and Pakistan. However, contrary to the assertions of some analysts, China no longer enjoys a privileged position in Myanmar's foreign policy as it had once enjoyed in the past. Although Myanmar benefited substantially from its relations with China in terms of political support, trade and military assistance,[21] the reform agenda allowed the country to mend its ties with the West and diversify its foreign relations, ending two decades of international isolation and pressure. This opened up new avenues for Myanmar's foreign partners, significantly increasing its bargaining leverage vis-à-vis China and reducing its dependence on the latter.[22] President Thein Sein now wants to bring China's two economic rivals—the US and Japan—into Myanmar in an apparent bid to offset two decades of Chinese dominance.[23] Nonetheless, opinions differ about the extent of the Chinese influence in Myanmar with views suggesting that Myanmar's foreign policy has not entirely diverged from that of China. Equally important for Myanmar in its policy of engagement with India is that it not only helps balance the country's excessive dependence on China but also helps boost its international standing and legitimacy.[24] With Myanmar's re-emergence onto the world stage, the potential for it to play an increased and more visible role in global affairs is significant.[25]

While Myanmar's democratic reforms are aimed at creating a political atmosphere conducive to bringing about a genuine reconciliation between the military and its political opponents, critics hold a view that the military in Myanmar maintains the country's control and has devised a system for improvement in human rights and other issues without letting the country become a full-fledged democracy which one can call a "modified democracy".[26] Some even claim that the democratic reform programme in Myanmar is nothing but a "smokescreen" for continued military rule. Many others, however, insist that the transformation is change-driven and that the measures that have been adopted in Myanmar, however small and tentative, cannot be discounted.[27]

## The Bangladesh–Myanmar Relationship in a New Setting

In the eyes of Bangladesh, the political transition and economic reconstruction process in Myanmar are impressive and encouraging. The dramatic transition leading to Myanmar's opening to the external world is indicative of an opportunity to recalibrate the Bangladesh–Myanmar ties. Bangladesh, as a neighbour and a major stakeholder, needs to respond to and adjust with the changes in Myanmar. Indeed, Myanmar's reform programme has engendered a new relationship with Bangladesh.

The central question is: with Myanmar moving forward on the road to democratic reforms and with the domestic power equations changing perceptibly, how best and most effectively can Bangladesh seize this opportunity and promote its relations with Myanmar? In its relations with the countries in South Asia, Myanmar seeks to advance several political, economic and strategic interests. At the broadest level, Myanmar's current policy towards South Asia helps to promote its overall diplomatic strategy of establishing a more peaceful and constructive external environment beyond Southeast Asia while carrying an image of Myanmar as a prospective regional player. The liberalisation and opening up of the country's economy is a clear manifestation of this foreign policy choice. Moreover, in launching and shaping the new foreign policy agenda, Myanmar has demonstrated its regional leadership capacity and determination to contribute constructively in allaying tensions and promoting mutual benefits. Myanmar's emergence in regional affairs adds a new dimension to the geopolitical and geostrategic calculus in the Asia-Pacific region and the country's opening provides a unique opportunity and rationale for Bangladesh to chart a new bilateral relationship.

The democratic reforms in Myanmar necessitate the country to seek more cooperation and understanding with its neighbours including Bangladesh. The non-settlement of the maritime boundary dispute between the two countries had plagued the bilateral relationship for long. However, in 2012, the International Tribunal for the Law of the Sea (ITLOS), a Hamburg-based independent judicial body, delivered its ruling on the delimitation of the maritime boundaries between Bangladesh and Myanmar in the Bay of Bengal. The verdict sustained Bangladesh's claim to a full Exclusive Economic Zone (EEZ) in the Bay of Bengal and a major part of the outer continental shelf beyond the EEZ. The judgment satisfied both the parties as it settled a long-running dispute over fishing rights and most importantly, the right to explore the seabed for oil, gas and mineral resources. Beyond doubt, the ITLOS-adjudicated settlement of this conflict between Bangladesh and Myanmar has effectively removed one of the major stumbling blocks in the bilateral relationship. After the delimitation of their maritime boundaries, a comfort level has been reached that allows both Dhaka and Naypyidaw to start cooperation on a number of outstanding issues and both have adopted a pragmatic foreign policy orientation in that direction. Obviously, the settlement of the maritime boundary dispute has changed the past conditions and understanding, leading to a more harmonious and cooperative relationship between the two countries. In comparison to the past, Bangladesh's bilateral relations with Myanmar have now gained a more stable footing with a prospect of further development and expansion.

The political and economic value of Bangladesh–Myanmar relations is undeniable and this bilateral relationship draws tremendous policy attention in both countries. The conspicuous reforms in Myanmar explain the level of optimism for a better Bangladesh–Myanmar cooperation and understanding. Matters relating to preferences, priorities and policy responses in coping with the changes in Myanmar will bring into question Bangladesh's ability to maintain a well-balanced policy and strategy that would dictate the Bangladesh–Myanmar relations in future. Indeed, Bangladesh pursues a coherent and consistent policy towards Myanmar that has transcended different administrations. A broad spectrum of the country's officials and nongovernmental actors consider Myanmar an emerging regional player. In one way or another, Myanmar has substantial political value as a reforming country and both Bangladesh and Myanmar need to derive the full utility and benefit of the relationship. Major political parties in Bangladesh—across the ideological divide and diverse social landscapes—are strong and enthusiastic supporters of the country's having better understanding and collaboration with Myanmar.[28] Moreover, a major segment of the Bangladeshi public opinion considers Myanmar's reform process and its growing economic power coupled with regional influence as just and reasonable.

To varying degrees, a new generation of people in Bangladesh is in favour of reaching a positive and constructive understanding with Myanmar. They offer some new and interesting considerations for Bangladesh–Myanmar relations. In their estimate, the importance of national interest and a realistic foreign policy is undeniable while Bangladesh is pursuing its relations with a reforming and changing Myanmar. In fact, their views suggest that Myanmar is now moving from a direct military rule to a form of "limited" or "guided democracy". Although a somewhat negative stereotype of Myanmar as a 'democracy deficient' country persists among the Bangladeshi populace, they contend that Myanmar's political system should not be allowed to hinder the future course of the bilateral relations. By this logic, Bangladesh should not squander the opportunity to improve its ties with an open and reforming Myanmar.[29] Arguments also run along the line that in the contemporary world, economic relations increasingly shape the contours of political relations and thus Bangladesh needs to work for building a better relationship not only with Myanmar's government but also with the country's democratic opposition and the civil society groups.

## Limitations of and Challenges to the Bilateral Relationship

Although Bangladesh–Myanmar relationship has witnessed considerable advances in the recent years, it remains difficult at times exposing the political sensitivities and disagreements on a few outstanding problems. Over the past several years, Bangladesh's relations with Myanmar have been punctuated by a few obstacles. But, it would be misleading to posit that the bilateral relations have become captive to irritants since the problems between the two countries are not necessarily deep-seated as many of them stem from insufficient interaction with and knowledge of each other. However, Bangladesh has evidently been keen to avert a situation leading to the aggravation of relations. Dhaka has pursued a number of objectives vis-à-vis Naypyidaw—by building better bilateral trade relations, supporting the country's political and economic transformation, building mutual confidence and resolving the conflicts/ tensions amenable to compromise.

Bangladesh calls attention to at least two/three obstacles in its relationship with Myanmar. Dhaka stresses that the reasons for convergence on those issues with Naypyidaw outweigh those of divergence. First, the question of the status of the Rohingya Muslims—who are a stateless minority groups in the Myanmarese society—over and over again puts the two neighbours at odds with one another; second, cross-border crime and terrorism often vitiate the ties, and finally, border tensions fuel mutual misunderstanding and distrust.

***Rohingya Question and National Security Concerns:*** Certain ethnic policies of the Myanmar government had led to large-scale infiltration of Rohingyas into Bangladesh in three phases: during 1978, 1991–92 and in 2012. Most analysts note that while the political and economic reforms are sweeping Myanmar, accusations of human rights abuses and ethnic unrest/violence in few states are challenging the country's reform efforts. President Thein Sein's administration sought reconciliation with Myanmar's different ethnic groups including those in the Rakhine (previously known as Arakan) province, home to the Rohingya Muslim minority, who have been fleeing their homeland in search of asylum in the predominantly Muslim countries like Bangladesh, Malaysia and Indonesia to escape discrimination, targeted violence and poverty. Bangladesh has always been their natural refuge in times of crises.[30] The Myanmar government claims that the Rohingyas are immigrants from the neighbouring Bangladesh which the latter vehemently denies and argues that they should be repatriated. A 1982 Citizenship Act of Myanmar excluded the Rohingya Muslims from the country's official list of 135 ethnic communities, leaving them stateless. The Myanmar government refuses to recognise the Rohingya Muslims making a case that the members of any officially recognised ethnic group must prove that their ancestors had lived in Myanmar before the British colonised the Arakan (Rakhine) area in 1823. Many Rohingyas say that their ancestors had lived in Myanmar for generations but the backward minority group lacks the documentation to prove it.[31] Actually, the ethno-religious character of the problem bars the conclusion of an agreement between Bangladesh and Myanmar to find a durable solution to the crisis.[32]

On the other hand, Bangladesh disowns the Rohingyas on legitimate grounds and has thus denied them refugee status since 1992.[33] Currently, Bangladesh hosts 28,000 registered/documented and between 200,000 and 500,000 unregistered/undocumented Rohingya refugees.[34] Although Bangladesh is not a signatory to the 1951 Refugee Convention, it has granted asylum to these refugees for a long time considering the humanitarian aspect of the problem and also the prospect of repatriation of the refugees to Myanmar. In fact, no national system is in place in Bangladesh to provide them with protection and support.

As the experience of many refugee-hosting nations indicates, refugees inevitably cause serious socio-economic, political, environmental and even cultural difficulties for the host countries. They reside in host countries for prolonged periods, leaving adverse impacts on the host communities. Likewise, the massive flow of the Rohingya refugees into Bangladesh continues to pose major problems of food, health, accommodation, employment, access to land and business opportunities. The worst result is that all these problems, in turn, jeopardise the public order and national security in Bangladesh. For instance, in response to the Myanmar government's repressive policies, several Rohingya armed groups have emerged in the recent decades which include the Rohingya Solidarity Organization (RSO) and the Arakan Rohingya Islamic Front (ARIF), both of which in 1996 jointly formed the Rohingya National Alliance (RNA). They operate from small bases in the Bangladesh–Myanmar border areas.[35]

Additionally, there is a serious allegation that the Rohingya refugee camps in the Cox's Bazar area are fanning Islamist militancy in Bangladesh and to much of Bangladesh's concerns, there is a growing militancy amongst a section of the refugees under the leadership of the RSO, an anti-Myanmar militant outfit created in order to safeguard the Rohingya interests,[36] which is suspected to have links with terrorist groups like the Jamaatul Mujahideen Bangladesh (JMB) and the Harkat-ul-Jihad-al-Islam (HuJI).[37] On the other hand, there are allegations from Myanmar that Bangladesh is harbouring Rohingya separatists,[38] although the Bangladeshi side plays this down on the ground of lack of any concrete evidence.

On a sinister note, the presence of the Rohingya refugees has changed the demographic character and ethnic complexion of parts of south-eastern Bangladesh (more specifically, Teknaf in the district of Cox's Bazar) where the Rohingyas stand a possibility of outnumbering the local population in the near future.

Another extremely important national security concern—which has been cited most often recently—is the role of the Rohingyas in passport forgery cases in Bangladesh which is a serious criminal offence. Media reports run stories of how hundreds of Rohingya refugees, trained in militancy, collect fake or forged Bangladeshi passports using false identities and travel to Middle Eastern countries mainly Saudi Arabia and United Arab Emirates, the United Kingdom and India for jobs and for various other purposes. Many of them get arrested in those countries for orchestrating unlawful and criminal activities that badly dent the image and credibility of Bangladesh while damaging the prospect of an expanded labour market in the Middle East.[39] With this national security concern in mind and also with the intention of controlling and regulating the activities of the Rohingyas living in Bangladesh, the Bangladesh government has recently banned marriages between Rohingya refugees and Bangladeshi nationals as the former use marriage certificates to claim Bangladeshi citizenship and passports.[40] An organised network involves the Rohingyas in preparing fake passports and thus the police verification process has been tightened to weed out the use of fraudulent passports. It is often much easier for the Rohingyas to acquire forged "breeder documents" while applying for Bangladeshi passports. The breeder document fraud is a practice in which a passport applicant presents fraudulent primary documents—such as driver's license, birth certificates or school identification cards—which can be used to establish necessary identification to eventually acquire a valid passport from the official passport-issuing authority. This type of passport fraud remains a key vulnerability in Bangladesh's national security system.

Myanmar is currently under mounting pressure from the global community to grant citizenship or at least provide strong legal protection to its Rohingya population. There has been large-scale influx of the Rohingya refugees from Myanmar to a few ASEAN countries too, like Malaysia and Thailand. The US President Barack Obama recently called on Myanmar to draft new plans to confer citizenship to the Rohingyas while a number of Western policymakers and analysts have suggested a 'blanket citizenship' for the Rohingyas in Myanmar, but neither President Thein Sein nor the NLD leader Aung San Suu Kyi have supported this proposal.[41] Of late, Myanmar has discarded a 2013 UN resolution urging it to confer citizenship to the Rohingyas.[42]

***Cross-Border Crime and Terrorism:*** The porous/fluid borders between Bangladesh and Myanmar engender cross-border organised criminal and terrorist activities that trigger strategic and tactical planning responses by the Bangladeshi government. Few of such illegal activities straddle the unpatrolled and unmonitored areas of the borders and involve smuggling, illicit trafficking of small arms/light weapons, narcotic drugs and human beings, especially women and children. Bangladesh is a major destination for illegal drugs originating in Myanmar and a thriving illegal trade in arms and drugs focused around the border town of Teknaf.[43] It has been found that the unregistered Rohingyas are involved/recruited as carriers, intermediaries or traffickers in the entire process.[44] Another troubling trend is the involvement of the Rohingya human traffickers from Bangladesh who allegedly traffic people to Malaysia.[45] Overall, cross-border criminal networks/activities carried out by the Rohingyas are undermining local security and governance, with highly negative impact on the economic activities and growth, rule of law, human rights and the societal and cultural advancement in the affected areas.

***Border Tensions and Skirmishes*:** Border tensions between Bangladesh and Myanmar flare up on occasions resulting in the killing of the members of the border security forces and innocent people. Several rounds of border talks have been held between the Border Guard Bangladesh (BGB) and Myanmar's Border Guard Police (BGP) aimed at securing and stabilising the borders. In recent times, Myanmar has started putting up a barbed wire fence in the Rakhine State, along its borders with Bangladesh. The fence will run along the 210 km land border between the two countries and will also stretch along the maritime border of the Naaf River passing through Maungdaw in the Rakhine province.[46] The Myanmarese government claims that the fencing project is critical to the country's security and it is intended to curb cross-border narcotic and human trafficking. In fact, a spate of ethnic disturbance and violence in the Rakhine state in 2012 has undermined border security and prompted the Myanmarese forces to beef up security at the borders. Critics say that the fencing of borders will hurt cross-border economy, send a wrong message to the people of Bangladesh and will produce mistrust and acrimony in bilateral relations. As both Dhaka and Naypyidaw understand the importance of diluting border tensions and jointly promote a well-managed, stable, peaceful and business-friendly environment.

## Promises in the Relationship: Sectors of Mutual Benefit

Overall, Myanmar's new diplomatic manoeuvring and trade and economic opportunities provide a strong logic and foundation for a mutually beneficial relationship and understanding. In Bangladesh's foreign policy community, Myanmar is treated as an important partner, and managing and improving ties with this south-eastern neighbour is one of the foremost foreign policy goals/challenges for the country. Within much of Bangladesh's business and political elites/luminaries—and the wider public—there is a continued sense of realisation of the importance of the country's improving relations with Myanmar. The following are the sectors in which both parties could derive reciprocal benefits.

***Trade and Business Opportunities***: The Bangladeshi Prime Minister Sheikh Hasina has been pursuing a pragmatic, rational and growth-oriented foreign policy. To be sure, the current state of the Bangladesh–Myanmar trade and commercial relations is below its full potential. One study shows that the current bilateral trade volume between Bangladesh and Myanmar is about $150 million, of which border trade represents $ 9 million.[47] According to another study in 2012-13, trade between Bangladesh and Myanmar reached around $ 100 million. During this period Bangladesh's exports to Myanmar stood at $ 13.67 million and imports were valued at $ 84 million. In comparison to 2011–2012, the imports from Myanmar climbed to $ 30 million and the exports from Bangladesh rose to only $ 0.27 million.[48] Although the once robust cross-border trade between Bangladesh and Myanmar is currently on the decline, Dhaka and Naypyidaw can restart the process for mutual gains.

As a changing and reforming Myanmar courts foreign investments in the country, the business climate there brings opportunities for the Bangladeshi investors as well. The Bangladeshi business community, particularly that which is interested in investing in Myanmar, can be encouraged. In the recent times, Bangladeshi entrepreneurs have shown an interest in investing in Myanmar, mainly in the agro-processing industries.[49]

***Cross-Border Connectivity:*** Even though Bangladesh is Myanmar's next-door neighbour, there is no direct connectivity between these two countries. In the past, such a connectivity included connecting Chittagong with the former Arakan state of Myanmar through a road link until the 1960s but later it was discontinued. Much to the optimism in Bangladesh, the two parties signed a Memorandum of Understanding (MoU) in 2007 to establish a direct road link between Bangladesh and Myanmar—now known as the Friendship Road—for boosting trade and economic growth. There was a proposal from Bangladesh for the construction of a 25-km road—2 km in Bangladesh and 23 km in Myanmar. Under the plan, the 2 km road would run through Balukhali–Gundhum on the Bangladeshi side and 23 km through the Gundum-Bawlibazar/Taungbro inside Myanmar.[50] Considering the tremendous importance of this road link which would facilitate connectivity with the Asian Highway and Kunming of the Yunnan province of China, the Bangladeshi government proposed to finance the road construction on the Myanmarese side too. The 2-km long Bangladesh-Myanmar Friendship Road would also facilitate the proposed Bangladesh-China-India-Myanmar (BCIM) economic corridor. The project is expected to be the largest multi-nation transport corridor in the subcontinent.[51] During the latest Foreign Office Consultation (FOC) at the secretary level between Bangladesh and Myanmar in 2014, both sides agreed to continue the project.[52]

In recognition of the importance of such connectivity, Myanmar is also making efforts at the broader level to strengthen the country's physical connectivity with its neighbours and explore its immensely advantageous geoeconomic position. On June 5, 2013, President Thein Sein stated:

> With China to our northeast, India and Bangladesh to our west, the other nations of ASEAN to our south and east, we border more than two billion people and the fastest growing markets in the world. Our country, once isolated not just by politics but by physical barriers, is now poised to break those barriers. We are becoming the door to Asia.[53]

While supporting Myanmar's regional approach, Dhaka views its relations with Naypyidaw from the standpoint of mutual exchange and interest.

***Energy Cooperation*:** Better known as the 'master resource' access to energy resources has emerged as a challenging concern for powers, big and small. Energy issues cannot be divorced from domestic politics and foreign policy.

With over 150 million people, Bangladesh is an energy-starved country and lacks a long-term energy security policy. In contrast, Myanmar is now believed to possess the tenth-largest natural gas reserves in the world, estimated at 90 trillion cubic feet.[54] Moreover, Myanmar has abundant reserves of around 600 million barrels of oil and 88 trillion cubic feet of natural gas.[55] Hence, an improved bilateral relationship with Myanmar would be conducive to meeting Bangladesh's quest for energy. The tri-nation India-Bangladesh-Myanmar gas pipeline project is seen as a strategically viable scheme for Bangladesh and recently the country has shown an interest in reviving the project and in the event of its implementation, a cooperative relationship with Myanmar would be of benefit to Bangladesh. Additionally, Bangladesh can import hydroelectric power from Myanmar in the future.

***People-to-People Contact***: Friendship and cooperation between Bangladesh and Myanmar should not only remain as a governmental prerogative—it has to flourish in people-to-people contacts and exchanges as both nations have a common history, culture and tradition to share. People-to-people contact is a powerful tool of diplomacy which can help shape and mould public opinion in favour of building stronger ties and trust and understanding between nations. Since 2011, there has not been a healthy flow of people between Bangladesh and Myanmar as most agree that the full potential of Bangladesh's ties with Myanmar cannot be attained without engaging journalists, scholars/academics, lawyers, students, businesspeople, artists and others from the civil society and Non-Governmental Organisation (NGO) community. In addition, people-to-people contact should be promoted through cultural exchanges, sports, education, trade fairs and the like. This needs to be expanded through a blend of new mechanisms, resources and sustained resilience. In the recent months, the Myanmar Institute of Strategic and International Studies (MISIS)—a prominent think tank from Myanmar—has been in frequent interaction and exchange with similar research institutes in Bangladesh like the Bangladesh Institute of International and Strategic Studies (BIISS), Bangladesh Enterprise Institute (BEI) and the Center for Policy Dialogue (CPD). Such an academic and research collaboration between the two countries will inevitably produce better ties.

## Looking Ahead

The account of the Bangladesh–Myanmar relations in the past four decades does not give us much room for satisfaction and optimism. Although Bangladesh and Myanmar have sporadically accumulated grievances and bitter experiences, it would be hard to state that the relationship has not yielded anything beneficial for the two sides. Both parties have acknowledged how important it is to nurture the bilateral relationship and both understand the importance of this partnership to encompass shared economic gains as well as political cooperation. Lately, Bangladesh's perceptions of Myanmar have undergone considerable change and Bangladesh needs to keep up with Myanmar's new political realities. Bangladesh emphasises the centrality of the "Look East" policy in its foreign relations and Myanmar can become an integral part of this policy.

Myanmar remains a priority for Bangladesh's foreign policy establishment. A reforming, more open and stable Myanmar now presents better opportunities to address the legitimate concerns of Bangladesh. Therefore, Bangladesh needs to set out a new direction in its policy toward Myanmar. The country needs to craft a clear and definitive plan to advance its future relations with Myanmar. Maintaining a balanced, beneficial and constructive relationship between the two countries will be a challenging task. An astute combination of dynamism and resilience will be required on the part of Bangladesh as Myanmar's external relations are also poised to change significantly.

Bangladesh and Myanmar enjoy a long-lasting bilateral relationship with a multi-layered and cross-ideological support in Bangladesh. Hence, the nature of this relationship has been pragmatic and mostly non-ideological. Compared to Bangladesh's relations with other South Asian countries, this relationship is the least politicised. As a result, there is solid and broad support in Bangladesh—ranging from the business community to the political parties in government and the opposition—for an advancement of collaboration with Myanmar. Politicians and common people in Bangladesh do not apparently have any anti-Myanmar sentiment or hatred. Rather, the Bangladeshi public opinion welcomes Myanmar's engagement with the international community and the country is portrayed in Bangladesh as a growing economic power and a future democracy. Today, major global players have growing stakes in Myanmar and hence, any kind of acrimony or confrontation with Myanmar would be far too costly for Bangladesh to bear.

## Concluding Remarks

By and large, relations between Bangladesh and Myanmar have been friendly and cooperative. As a matter of fact, Myanmar's burgeoning foreign relations, coupled with its international recognition, and its growing regional role, call for a new Bangladesh–Myanmar understanding and collaboration—one that breaks out of past difficulties and promises to expand more. Although the current level of cooperation between them is less than fully satisfactory, the relative value of the bilateral relationship has increased with the gradual shaping of a much more competitive regional environment. Despite the presence of a few irritants, both Dhaka and Naypyidaw share such a relationship that can neither afford to derail the partnership by any act of underestimation nor by any miscalculation of the reality. Indeed, the bilateral relationship has weathered a few crises in the last two decades and it has been driven and shaped by mutual interest and necessity. From a realistic point of view, the advent of a new civilian government in Myanmar and the developments in Bangladesh present a window of opportunity for both the countries to pursue an innovative approach to nurture the mutually beneficial relationship. In the changing regional environment, Bangladesh should skilfully navigate the challenges of its relations with Myanmar and a more inclusive and effective diplomacy on both sides can win them significant places in each other's foreign policy calculations. All things considered, extensive scholarly interpretation and analysis of Bangladesh-Myanmar relations can better inform the perspectives of the both sides that have much riding on an equitable, stable and productive bilateral relationship.

## NOTES

1. The two countries share a common border of 314.40 km including 207. 20 km of land border, 68.20 km of the Naaf River and 39.00 km of maritime boundary in the strategic waters of the Bay of Bengal. See for details, M. Jashim Uddin, "Prospects for Attaining a New Height in Bangladesh-Myanmar Relations: Bangladesh Perspective", *BIISS Journal*, Vol. 35, No. 1 (January 2014), p. 1.
2. Zahedul Amin, "Changing Dynamics in Myanmar Impact Bangladesh's Geopolitics", *The Diplomat*, June 23, 2014. Available at: http://thediplomat.com/2014/06/changing-dynamics-in-myanmar-impact-bangladeshs-geopolitics/
3. Catharin Dalpino, "Second Chance: Prospects for U.S.-Myanmar Relations" in Mely Caballero-Anthony and others (eds.), *Myanmar's Growing Regional Role* (Washington: National Bureau of Asian Research, 2014), p. 34.
4. Jashim Uddin, "Prospects for Attaining a New Height in Bangladesh-Myanmar Relations: Bangladesh Perspective", p. 4.
5. Harun ur Rashid, *Bangladesh Foreign Policy: Realities, Priorities and Challenges* (Dhaka: Academic Press and Publishers, 2012), p. 186.
6. "Mynamar-Bangladesh Bilateral Relations". Embassy of the Republic of the Union of Myanmar (Dhaka, Bangladesh). Available at: http://www.myanmarembassydhaka.com/myanmar-bangladesh-bilateral-relations-2/
7. Lee Jones, "Explaining Myanmar's Regime Transition: The Periphery is Central", *Democratization*, Vol. 21, No, 5, 2014, pp. 780-802, here p. 781.

8. Ibid.
9. Udai Bhanu Singh, "Do the Changes in Myanmar Signify a Real Transition?", *Strategic Analysis*, Vol. 37, No. 1, January-February 2013, p. 101.
10. Amin, "Changing Dynamics in Myanmar Impact Bangladesh's Geopolitics".
11. Ibid.
12. *"Myanmar: No Turning Back"*. Available at: *www.countrystrategic.com/pdf/Myanmar_Complete.pdf*
13. Ibid.
14. Asian Development Bank (ADB), *Myanmar in Transition: Opportunities and Challenges* (Manila: Asian Development Bank, 2012), p. vii.
15. IMF, "World Economic and Financial Surveys". Available at http://www.imf.org/external/pubs/ft/weo/2011/02/weodata/index.aspx
16. Joshua Brown, "A Fertile Land", *Southeast Asia Globe*, December 14, 2012. Available at: http://sea-globe.com/a-fertile-land/
17. Trevor Wilson, "Foreign Policy as a Political Tool: Myanmar 2003-2006" in Monique Skidmore & Trevor Wilson (eds.), *Myanmar: The State, Community and the Environment* (Canberra: Australian National University Press, 2007), p. 84.
18. In 2006, Myanmar was forced to relinquish the rotating chairmanship of ASEAN in order to avoid a damaging Western boycott of the bloc's meetings. In fact, when Myanmar joined ASEAN in 1997, the country's membership was met with strong resistance from the West because of its 'poor' human rights record under the military rule.
19. The World Economic Forum on East Asia (WEF-EA) is an Asian equivalent of the Davos World Economic Forum (WEF).
20. Aung Tun, "Is China Being Sidelined?", *The Diplomat*, June 26, 2013. Available at: http://thediplomat.com/2013/06/myanmars-look-west-policy-is-china-being-sidelined/
21. Jürgen Haacke, *Myanmar's Foreign Policy: Domestic Influences and International Implications*, Adelphi Papers, No. 381, 2006, p. 28.
22. Yun Sun, "China's Relations with Myanmar: National Interests and Uncertainties" in Jung-Ho Bae and Jae H. Ku (eds.), *China's Internal and External Relations and Lessons for Korea and Asia* (Seoul: Korean Institute for National Unification, 2013), p. 283.
23. Tun, "Is China Being Sidelined?" *The Diplomat*, June 26, 2013.
24. Haacke, *Myanmar's Foreign Policy: Domestic Influences and International Implications*, p. 37.
25. Meredith Miller and Abraham M. Denmark, "Introduction: Myanmar's Re-emergence" in Mely Caballero-Anthony and others (eds.), *Myanmar's Growing Regional Role* (Washington: National Bureau of Asian Research, 2014), p. 3.
26. Pek Koon Heng, "Myanmar in ASEAN: Opportunities and Challenges Ahead for the 2014 ASEAN Chair", *ASEAN Studies Center Report*, (Washington, D.C.: American University, 2013), p.12.
27. Thaung Tun, "European Union-Myanmar Relations in a Changing World: Time for Paradigm Shift" in Nick Cheesman, Monique Skidmore & Trevor Wilson

(eds.), *Myanmar's Transition: Openings, Obstacles and Opportunities* (Singapore: Institute of Southeast Asian Studies, 2012), p. 288.

28. Based on the author's conversations/interviews with a few leaders of mainstream political parties in Bangladesh.
29. The author's personal communications with students from different public and private universities in Bangladesh.
30. Partha S. Ghosh, "South Asia's Response to Its Refugee Questions" in Siegfried O. Wolf et al (eds.), *Politics in South Asia: Culture, Rationality and Conceptual Flow* (New York & London: Springer, 2015), p. 116.
31. "Burma Constructs New Border Checkpoints with Bangladesh", March 20, 2014. Available at: http://www.voanews.com/content/burma-constructs-new-border-checkpoints-with-bangladesh/1875708.html
32. Partha S. Ghosh, "South Asia's Response to Its Refugee Questions", p. 116.
33. Reuters, "Myanmar Rejects UN Resolution on Rohingya Muslims", November 21, 2013. Available at: http://www.reuters.com/article/2013/11/21/us-myanmar-rohingya-un-idUSBRE9AK0P120131121. See also, Amin, "Changing Dynamics in Myanmar Impact Bangladesh's Geopolitics".
34. Jashim Uddin, "Prospects for Attaining a New Height in Bangladesh-Myanmar Relations: Bangladesh Perspective", p. 4.
35. Syed Serajul Islam, "State Terrorism in Arakan" in Andrew T.H. Tan (ed.), *A Handbook of Terrorism and Insurgency in Southeast Asia* (Northampton, MA: Edward Elgar Publishing Inc., 2007), pp. 339-340.
36. Gautam Sen, "Border Tension between Bangladesh and Myanmar", *IDSA Comment*, August 24, 2014.
37. Partha S. Ghosh, "South Asia's Response to Its Refugee Questions", p. 116.
38. Amin, "Changing Dynamics in Myanmar Impact Bangladesh's Geopolitics".
39. Md. Rasooldeen, "Rohingyas Using Fake Passports to Reach KSA", *Arab News*, April 15, 2013. Also, Shudipta Sharma, "Fake Passports: 16 Rohingyas Held at Airport", *The Daily Star*, August 30, 2012.
40. C.R. Abrar, "Marriage Ban on Rohingyas", *The Daily Star*, July 16, 2014.
41. Catharin Dalpino, "Second Chance: Prospects for U.S.-Myanmar Relations" in Mely Caballero-Anthony and others (eds.), *Myanmar's Growing Regional Role* (Washington: National Bureau of Asian Research, 2014), p. 31.
42. Reuters, "Myanmar Rejects UN Resolution on Rohingya Muslims", November 21, 2013. Available at: http://www.reuters.com/article/2013/11/21/us-myanmar-rohingya-un-idUSBRE9AK0P120131121
43. Ewan W. Anderson, *International Boundaries: A Geopolitical Atlas* (London: Routledge, 2003), p. 577.
44. Bangladesh has long been worried about a huge inflow of smuggled contraband drugs like yaba, phensedyl, heroin, illegal alcohol and hemp from Myanmar. Bangladeshi officials say that large-scale illegal drugs, including contraband yaba tablets, are smuggled into the country through the hilly areas of the border, especially Teknaf in Cox's Bazar and Naikhongchhari in Banbardan. The 250-kilometre land border between Bangladesh and Myanmar is a hotspot for drug-smuggling between the countries. A high-profile monitoring committee comprising members of the border security forces and officials from different

anti-narcotic organisations, has been set up by Bangladesh to curb drug trafficking along the borders. See, "Bangladesh Seeks Talks with Myanmar to Check Drug Smuggling", *The Financial Express* (Dhaka), April 20, 2014.

45. Weena Kowitwanij, "Rohingya: Victims of Human Trafficking in Thailand", *Asia News*, February 5, 2015.
46. "Building Barriers: Fencing Off the Bangladesh Border", May 13, 2014. Available at: https://www.dvb.no/dvb-video/building-barriers-fencing-off-the-bangladesh-border/40644
47. Aspen Institute India, *India's Moment with Myanmar: The Promise and Challenges of a New Relationship* (Gurgaon: Aspen Institute India, 2012), p. 7.
48. Jashim Uddin, "Prospects for Attaining a New Height in Bangladesh-Myanmar Relations: Bangladesh Perspective", p. 11.
49. Ibid., p. 18.
50. Ibid., p. 10.
51. FHM Humayan Kabir, "Road Project to Connect Myanmar Sent to PC", *The Financial Express,* August 21, 2014.
52. Munima Sultana, "Friendship Road", *The Financial Express*, October 14, 2014.
53. Thein Sein, Address to the Young Global Leaders at the 22nd World Economic Forum on East Asia at Naypyidaw, June 5, 2013. Available at: http://m.president-office.gov.mm/en/?q=briefing-room/news/2013/06/06/id-2150
54. Gurmeet Kanwal, "A Strategic Perspective on India-Myanmar Relations" in Lex Rieffel (ed.), *Myanmar/Burma: Inside Challenges, Outside Interests* (Washington, D.C.: The Brookings Institution, 2010), p. 136.
55. Bibhu Prasad Routray, "India's Myanmar Policy: Rational Change" in V.R. Raghavan (ed.), *Internal Conflicts in Myanmar: Transnational Consequences* (New Delhi: Vij Books India Private Limited, 2011, p. 140).

# 10

# The India Factor in Sino-Myanmar Relations

*Yukteshwar Kumar*

Myanmar, as compared to the large countries in Asia, is smaller in area. But, its geographical and strategic location at a juncture above the Bay of Bengal sandwiched between Northeast India, Southern China and western Thailand makes it economically, politically and strategically a very significant nation in this region. It has a very long (approximately 1,930 km; compared to the Indian coastline of 7,517 km and the Chinese coastline of 14,500 km) coastline which further strengthens its significance and importance in the determination of regional politics.

China and Myanmar have long enjoyed historical and cultural closeness; the relationship between the two nations has been termed as 胞波 *Paukphaw* in Burmese and *Baobo* in Chinese meaning *Bhai–bhai* in the early 1950s. Myanmar was one of the earliest states in the world to establish diplomatic relationship with China even before India had recognised the People's Republic of China.[1]

The mutual relationship between the two countries has been based on the Five Principle of Peaceful Co-Existence—*Panchsheel*—and several top elites and leaders of both the countries have visited each other several times. The first Premier of China, Zhou Enlai (周恩来), visited Myanmar nine times and the former premier and head of state of Burma, Ne Win (also the founder of the Burma Socialist Programme Party), visited China several times. The bilateral relationship between the top leaders of both the countries has continued even in the recent times and almost all the top Chinese leaders including Jiang Zemin (江泽民), Hu Jintao (胡锦涛), Wen Jiabao (温家宝), Li Changchun (李长春) and Xi Jinping (习近平) have visited Myanmar.

After the new civilian government came to power in Myanmar, the Chairman of the Chinese People's Consultative Conference, Jia Qinglin (贾庆林) became the first foreign leader to visit Myanmar in April 2011. In reciprocation, President Thein Sein made a state visit to China in May 2011 and has been visiting the country every year since then. In September 2012 and May 2013, he visited China and went to Nanning (南宁) in the Guangxi (广西) province and also visited Shaanxi (陕西), Hainan (海南) and the Guangdong (广东) provinces. In June 2014, on the eve of the 60th anniversary of the *Panchsheel*, President Thein Sein again visited Beijing (北京) and apart from meeting top Chinese leaders he also met the Indian Vice President Dr Hamid Ansari and had cordial talks with all them.

But, the political relation between China and Myanmar has not been rosy always and in 1967 there were anti-Chinese riots in Burma and the Chinese communities were expelled from the country, which generated hostility between both the nations.[2] However during the military junta rule in Burma/Myanmar, China was the only major country in the world which openly supported Myanmar, locally and globally. China has extended diplomatic support to Myanmar on several occasions at various international forums when most of the developed nations in the world were busy criticising the country on its human rights record and had imposed civilian and military sanctions on it. China has given at the least $2 billion worth of arms to the country which includes fighter aircraft, patrol boats, tanks, armoured personnel carriers, multiple rocket launchers, artillery, communications equipment, small arms and ammunition.[3] The Burmese army has also received training from the Chinese army.

In this paper I seek to examine China's existing strategic relation with Myanmar and the role that India should play in the changing atmosphere after the general elections in Myanmar later this year. It also attempts to examine as to how the mishandling of the Sino-Myanmarese relations, arrogance, negligence and interference by the Chinese military in the internal affairs of Myanmar might shift the balance of Naypyidaw towards New Delhi rather than Beijing.

## Cultural Relationship between Myanmar and China

Apart from friendly and brotherly relationship between China and

Myanmar, people-to-people contact and a good bonhomie on the border areas have been persisting between the two nations since time immemorial. During the Tang (唐朝) Dynasty, it is reported that a Burmese king along with a big entourage visited the then Chinese capital of 西安). After independence, several cultural and artistic delegations from both the countries visited each other's nations. In January 1996, both the countries signed an agreement of cooperation in the art and cultural field in Beijing. It is said that Buddha's relics have been taken from China to various cities in Myanmar four times (1955, 1994, 1996 and 2011) which have been warmly received by the public in the country. The festival of *Boshuijie* (泼水节) (like Holi in India) has been celebrated jointly between China and Myanmar near Ruili (瑞丽) for more than 14 years since 2011.

However, in recent times, the 'anti-China' sentiment has been on the rise in Myanmar because many locals have seen the wealthy Chinese occupy their lands and exploit their natural resources. They are also accused of using only Chinese labour instead of the local labourers in laying down their projects. For instance, people from the Kachin province, the northern most state of Myanmar, are particularly unhappy with the government's decision of protecting the Chinese investors as against the demands of the locals.

China is also wary of the democratic rallies and the freedom of expression in Myanmar. It fears that through people-to-people contact, their clamour for democracy may reach inner China and that it will have severe implications and consequences for its homeland[4] as China is still a one-party state with the Communist Party of China well aware of the spread of the democratic voice from Myanmar to that of its own country.

## Myanmar and India

India and Myanmar share a very long border (approximately 1,600 km). Like China, India has a very long history of interface with Myanmar but unlike China, the Indian kings and emperors never subjugated Myanmar and it was never a vassal state of India. During the British colonial rule, Myanmar remained a part of their colony. India has enjoyed special relationship with Myanmar because of its cultural, ethnic, historical and religious linkages. Eighty nine percent of the Burmese people are Buddhist and follow the Theravada religious sect and for them , making a pilgrimage to Bodh Gaya in India is like a dream come true.. The ancient culture of the country including the *Pyu* culture was heavily influenced by the bilateral trade with India, which imported Buddhism as well as other cultural, architectural and political concepts that had an enduring influence on the later Burmese culture and political organisation.

Myanmar has two percent of the ethnic Indian population and three percent of the ethnic Chinese population residing within the country. Earlier, the Burmese government had expelled the Indians from the country as the Indian businessmen were wielding a negative impact upon the Burmese economy till its attainment of independence in 1948. Post-1980s, India was most critical of the suppression of the 1988 uprising and had closed down its borders and set up refugee camps in the vicinity to shelter pro-democratic supporters in the country.[5] The relationship continued to deteriorate further until the Indian Prime Minister Mr Rajiv Gandhi visited the country in 1987 that resulted in removing the bad blood between these two close yet estranged neighbours.

Immediately, trade and investment saw an upward swing, followed by the landslide victory of Daw Aung San Suu Kyi in the country's first general elections in 1990. But the military government in Burma refused to cede power, putting Suu Kyi under house arrest. India, in the meantime, gave a pragmatic push to its foreign policy and embarked on the Look East Policy in an attempt to:

> (a) search for stability in India's troubled Northeast region; (b) rope in the economic opportunities tendered by Burma and other ASEAN members; and (c) attempt to counterbalance China's growing regional presence in this area.

On the economic front, though, there is no denying the fact that China has embraced Myanmar quicker and more aptly than India.[6] The Indian constructive engagement with Myanmar has come after quite a bit of hesitation especially because of the military crackdown in the country. The bilateral trade between India and Myanmar is about $ 2.18 billion while the bilateral trade between China and Myanmar is over $ 5 billion and is growing consistently.[7]

The real opportunity for the Indian trade and economic relation with Myanmar comes now. There is a new government in India and the West has lifted all the civilian sanctions on Myanmar. Myanmar is at the crossroads to elect a new civilian government in October/November this year and in the backdrop of major competition from many other countries, India should compete for larger access to the Burmese markets. The current government under Prime Minister Narendra Modi has been popularly known as a 'pro-business' government and from the day of his inauguration, Modi has started to forge and cement concrete bilateral relationships with all the neighbouring countries, including Myanmar.[8]

Modi has equipped himself well in the sphere of diplomacy, and his emphasis on connectivity and the building of shared values with neighbours has a resonance in Myanmar's case. It remains to be seen whether he can sell India's strengths effectively and infuse the economic and strategic bilateral relationship with a much-needed dose of dynamism.[9]

Besides propagating the Act East policy, it has been reported that both the governments of India and Myanmar are closely working on a rail and road connectivity between the two sides. In January 2015, the newly elected government in New Delhi proposed the Imphal–Mandalaya bus service. Of the total length of the road in the two countries, the Imphal –Moreh section of NH-39 is 110 km, while on Myanmar's side, the distance between Moreh and Mandalay via Tamu town is 469 km.[10] The Indian and Myanmarese governments believe that the road will dramatically increase trade between the two remote regions on either side of the border at Moreh, and pave the way for greater investment as Myanmar strives to come out from decades of isolation under the military rule.[11] Although the opening of the road may trigger more drug trafficking, if concrete measures are taken to tackle the problem it can be controlled and the opening up of the roadways will then be in the interest of both the countries.

According to That Myint-U:

> "The amazing thing is that even though Burma and India were both part of the British Indian Empire, there was no proper road, no rail link, and pretty much no overland route connecting the two during the entire period of colonial rule...The overland route became a reality only in 1945 when the Ledo road was finally finished. This bus route is part of a much bigger historic turn that is taking place, a weaving together of the India, Burma, and China borderlands, and the creation of Burma as an Asian crossroads for the first time in history."[12]

Apart from the road link, there is a general understanding between India and Myanmar that their railways will be interconnected via a 346-km line section that will extend from Kalay in Myanmar to Jiribam in India via the border point at Tamu/Moreh, India. The rail link between Jiribam and Tapul/Imphal has been sanctioned by the Indian Railways, but that is unlikely to be completed before 2016. In 2011, construction work was in progress on a 97-kilometres stretch between Jiribam and Tupul/Imphal.[13] The UPA government was also supportive of this idea and eight years ago in 2007, India signed the inter-governmental agreement on the trans-Asian railway that is proposed to connect more than 25 countries.[14] The railway Board Chairman J.P. Batra signed the agreement at the United Nations

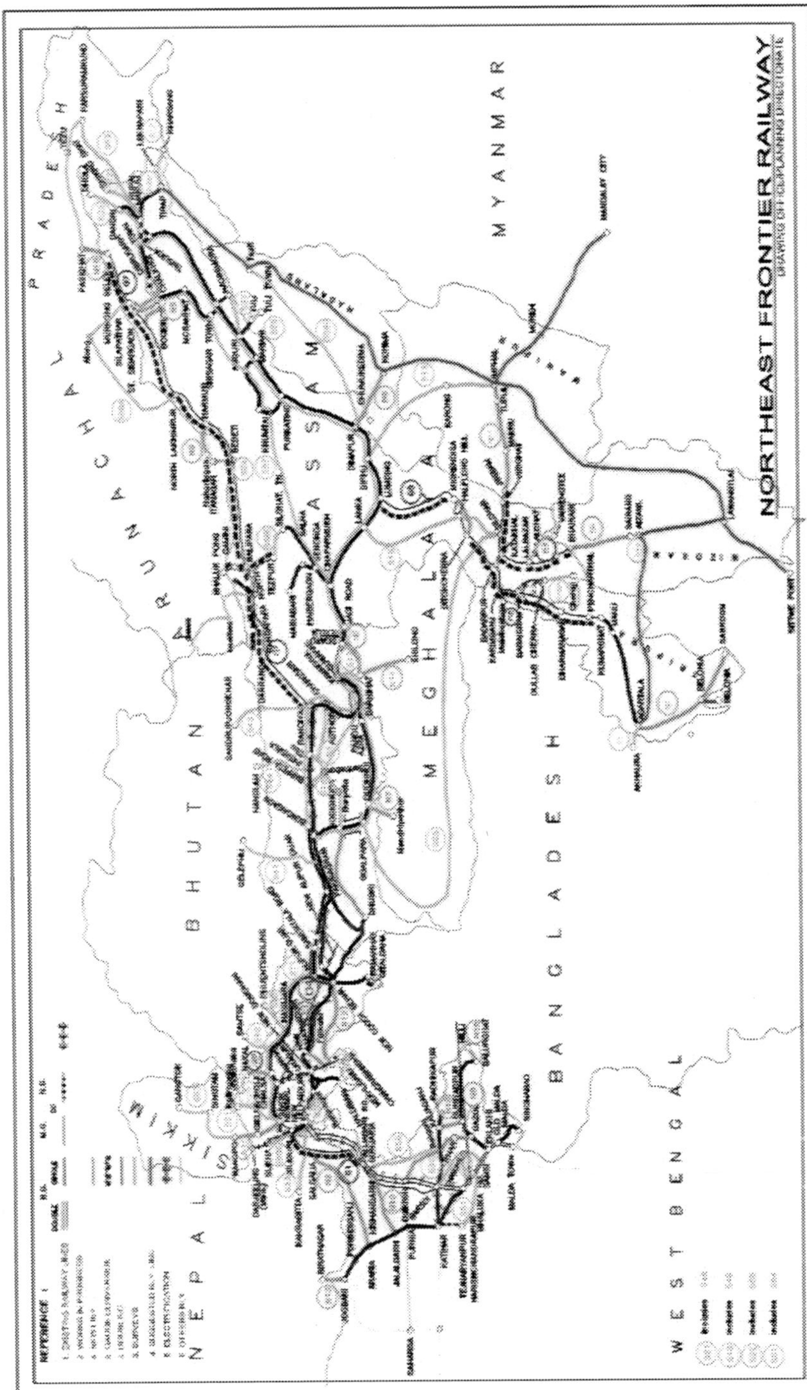


*Source:* Northeast Frontier Railway[16]

headquarters in New York. Earlier, 18 countries had signed it at Busan in Korea in November 2006. Now with India and Bangladesh signing it, 20 countries have become signatories.[15]

In the last two decades, India lost the opportunity to cement its ties with Myanmar while China edged it out during this period through its soft power, trade and economic ties in the region. India has some advantages over China, including the close cultural and religious affinity between Hinduism and Buddhism. The Indian democracy is also admired by the majority of Myanmar people while the Chinese are despised by many as the 'exploiter of their economy' and for making selfish benefit.[17]

## Aung San Suu Kyi

Daw Aung San Suu Kyi has a deep personal bonding and relationship with India. When her mother served as the Ambassador to India, she came along and studied at the Convent of Jesus and Mary School in New Delhi and graduated from the Lady Shri Ram College for Women in New Delhi with a degree in Political Science in 1964.[18] She also served as a Fellow at the Indian Institute of Advance Studies (IIAS), Shimla. In 1993, the Indian government conferred upon her the prestigious Jawaharlal Nehru Award for International Understanding.[19]

Aung San Suu Kyi is free today and under her leadership her party will contest the elections this year. However as she had been married to a foreigner in the past, the current 2008 Constitution of Myanmar still deters her from becoming the Head of the State in the country. The whole world, including the people in her own country, highly respect her and she will be the key person to watch in the future who could play a pivotal role in deciding the course of Myanmar and the future of its relationship with India and China.

## Conclusion

Currently, Myanmar's relations with both India and China are sound but with a tilt in the favour of China. The balance of the relationship is important for both India and China because of Myanmar's strategic location and the ambition of both the big nations to play a bigger role in Asian and international politics.

China wants to emerge as a very strong country with huge naval capacity and for this, Myanmar in the south is of great strategic importance. Many academicians have written in the past regarding the 'string of pearls' policy of China to encircle India, and Myanmar has to favour China in this. There have been reports of the construction of a large naval base for providing all kinds of support to the Chinese warships near the Hainggyi Island and India has raised concerns over this. The construction of the 'maritime facilities' being built by the Chinese on the Coco Islands which is just 45 km north of the Andaman Islands, is another concern for India. The intelligence equipment and the signal stations being built by the Chinese on these islands are causing a headache for the Indian observers there.

In comparison to India, China has invested very heavily in Myanmar and over 60 perent of the Foreign Direct Investment in Myanmar is from China. Myanmar is extremely important for the neighbouring landlocked Yunnan province of China and China will try its best that it does not lose the 'war of trade and business' vis-à-vis India.

Myanmar may attract China more for geopolitical and geoeconomic reasons but on the basis of geo-cultural and geo-civilisational reasons, India shall always have a leverage ahead of China. On the geostrategic grounds, both India and China shall compete against each other to get a better deal from Myanmar. Most of the Western nations including the USA would like India to have better ties with Myanmar rather than the Chinese having a closer relation with the country. As the US President Barack Obama in his recent speech while on a three-day visit to India said, "India can help Sri Lanka and Myanmar in the Asia Pacific region".[20]

As Ko Ko Thett wrote rightly in *The Irrawaddy* on 11 September, 2010: "Beijing's influence in Myanmar may be waning but its political leverage over Naypyidaw is still greater than that of the US and EU combined". No one country can deliberately choose its neighbours and both India and China would like to cajole Myanmar in the future, being its two biggest neighbouring nations. Given the mandate that the pro-business government in India has got now, it will be interesting to watch how India does business with Myanmar.

## NOTES

1. Toshihiro Kudo, "Myanmar's Economic Relations with China: Can China Support the Myanmar Economy?" Discussion Paper No. 66, Institute of Developing Economies, Japan, July 2006, see http://www.ide.go.jp/English/Publish/Download/Dp/pdf/066.pdf, (Accessed on 1 February 2015).
2. Geng Lixin, "Sino-Myanmar Relations: Analysis and Prospects" in *The Culture Mandala*, Vol. 7, no. 2, December 2006. http://www.international-relations.com/CM7-2WB/Sino-Myanmar.htm (Accessed on 1 February 2015).
3. Bertin Linter, "Chinese Arms Bolster Burmese Forces", *Jane's Defence Weekly*, 27 November 1993, p. 11.
4. 'Sino-Burmese Relation—Significance of Burmese Democracy in China-

中缅关系——缅甸民主化对中国的意义', *Radio Free Asia Website*, 8 October 2013, http://www.rfa.org/mandarin/zhuanlan/zhuantixilie/miandianminzhu-zhuanxing/burma-10082013095603.html (Accessed on 4 February 2015)

5. Europa Publications Staff, 2002, p. 872 &Lwin, NyiNyi, *Refugee Student Interviews*, A Burma-India Situation Report, 1992.
6. C. Raja Mohan, "PM Narendra Modi in Myanmar: Rebuilding the Historic Connections", *The Indian Express*, New Delhi, 14 November 2014 - See more at: http://indianexpress.com/article/opinion/columns/modi-in-myanmar-rebuilding-the-historic-connections (Accessed on 27 January 2015).
7. Sridhar Ramaswamy andTridivesh Singh Maini, "The Strategic Importance of Myanmar for India', *The Diplomat*, New Delhi, 12 August 2014 http://thediplomat.com/2014/08/the-strategic-importance-of-myanmar-for-india/ (Accessed on 3 February 2015).
8. Akhilesh Pillalamarri, "Why Was Myanmar's President Not Invited to Modi's Swearing-In Ceremony?" *The Diplomat*, New Delhi, 03 June 2014, See http://thediplomat.com/2014/06/why-was-myanmars-president-not-invited-to-modis-swearing-in-ceremony/ (Accessed on 11 January 2015).
9. Tridivesh Singh Maini, "India's 'Look East' Policy Begins with Myanmar", *The Diplomat*, New Delhi, 8 November 2014, See http://thediplomat.com/2014/11/indias-look-east-policy-begins-with-myanmar/ (Accessed on 1 February 2015).
10. "Survey on for Imphal-Mandalay Bus Service", *The Times of India*, New Delhi, 13 January 2015. See http://timesofindia.indiatimes.com/city/guwahati/Survey-on-for-Imphal-Mandalay-bus-service/articleshow/45859613.cms (Accessed on 19 January 2015).
11. Dean Nelson, "India to Reopen the Road to Mandalay", *The Telegraph*, London, 24 June, 2014, see http://www.telegraph.co.uk/news/10923164/India-to-reopen-the-Road-to-Mandalay.html (Accessed on 19January 2015).
12. Ibid.
13. Sandeep Joshi, "India Signs Accord on Trans-Asian Railway Network", *The Hindu*, Chennai, 1 July 2007, http://www.thehindu.com/todays-paper/tp-national/article1864234.ece (Accessed on 20 January 2015).
14. See *The Telegraph*, Kolkata, 26 February, 2011, http://www.telegraphindia.com/1110226/jsp/frontpage/story_13637652.jsp (Accessed on 12 January 2015).
15. Ibid.
16. See the map available on http://www.mdoner.gov.in/sites/default/files/silo3_content/railways/Railwaymap.pdf (Accessed on 1 February 2015).
17. In a personal interview with a Myanmarese scholar (who wishes to remain anonymous) at the University of Bath, UK on 1 February 2015.
18. Jesper Bengtsson, *Aung San Suu Kyi: A Biography*, Potomac Books, March 2012.
19. See *List of Jawaharlal Nehru Award* at http://www.iccrindia.net/jnawardlist.html (Accessed on 7 January 2015).
20. "Obama Promotes Religious Tolerance in India Speech", *The New Indian Express*, Chennai, 27 January 2015, http://www.newindianexpress.com/nation/Obama-Promotes-Religious-Tolerance-in-India-Speech/2015/01/27/article2639289.ece (Accessed on 27 January 2015).

## REFERENCE AND BIBLIOGRAPHY

A. Acharya, "Seeking Security in the Dragon's Shadow: China and Southeast Asia in the emerging Asian Order', *RSIS Working Paper No. 44,* Nanyang Technological University, Singapore.

Andrew Selth, 'Burma and the Strategic Competition between China and India", *The Journal of Strategic Studies,* Vol. 19, No. 2, June 1996.

Bertil Lintner, "Enter the Dragon", *Far Eastern Economic Review (FEER),* December 22, 1994.

Bruce Matthews, "Myanmar 2000, Beyond the Reach of International Relief?" *Southeast Asian Affairs,* Singapore: Institute of Southeast Asian Studies, 2001.

C.S. Kuppuswamy, "Sino-Myanmar Relation and its Impact on the region", available at http://indianstrategicknowledgeonline.com/web/_papers44_paper4357.pdf

G. Das, N. Bijoy Singh and C.J. Thomas, (eds.), *Indo-Myanmar Border Trade: Status, Problems and Potentials.* New Delhi: Ajansha Publishing House, 2005.

David Shambaugh, "China Engaging Asia", *International Security,* Vol. 29, No. 3, 2004.

David I. Steinberg and Hongwei Fan, "Modern China-Myanmar Relations: Dilemmas of Mutual Dependence", *Philosophy East and West,* 63: (2), 2013.

D. Devare, *India and Southeast Asia,* Singapore: Institute of Southeast Asian Studies, 2005.

Donald M. Seekins, "Burma-China Relations: Playing with Fire", *Asian Survey,* Vol. 37, No. 6, University of California Press, June 1997.

J. Mohan Malik, "China-India Relations in the Post-Soviet Era: The Continuing Rivalry", *China Quarterly,* No. 142, June 1995.

J. Mohan Malik, "Sino- Indian Rivalry in Myanmar: Implications for Regional Security", *Contemporary Southeast Asia,* Vol. 16, No. 2, September 1994.

Toshiro Kudo, "Myanmar's Economic Relations with China: Can China Support the Myanmar Economy?" *Institute of Developing Economies Discussion Paper No. 66,* July 2006.

Marry P. Callahan, "New Dragon or Still Dragging?" *Asian Survey,* Vol. 35, No. 2, February 1995.

N. Ganesan, "Myanmar–China Relations: Interlocking Interests but Independent Output", *Japanese Journal of Political Science* 12(1): 95-111, 2011.

Poon Kim Shee, "The Political Economy of China-Myanmar Relations: Strategic and Economic Dimensions", *Ritsumeikan Annual Review of International Studies,* Vol. 1, 2002.

Poon Kim, "The South China Sea in China's Strategic Thinking", *Contemporary Southeast Asia,* Vol. 19, No. 4, March 1998.

Robert H. Taylor, *The State in Burma,* Honolulu: University of Hawaii Press, 1987.

S.D. Muni, *China's Strategic Engagement with the New ASEAN: An Exploratory Study of China's Post-Cold War Political, Strategic and Economic Relations with Myanmar, Laos, Cambodia and Vietnam,* Singapore: Institute of Defence and Strategic Studies, 2002.

Tin Maung Maung Than, "Myanmar and China: A Special Relationship", *Southeast Asian Affairs (2003),* pp.189-210.

余定邦 Yu Ding Bang, 《中缅关系史》 *History of Sino-Myanmar Relationship,* 光明日报出版社, 2000.

# Conclusion

*Amrita Dey*

The elections had been of prime focus in Myanmar this year. And as events had unfolded in the country it was no less enigmatic and adventurous than the one that had taken place there after the 1990s. Outstanding among the issues were the omission of Daw Aung San Suu Kyi as a candidate for President for the elections. According to most observers it was so because the military dominated political establishment had refused to amend clauses in the 2008 Constitution that prohibited Suu Kyi from becoming the head of the state. However, in a television interview (in India), Daw Suu expressed her wish to lead the country and turn it into a vibrant democracy, without elaborating on the question whether she wanted to be the President of the country or not.[1]

Second, involved the developments within the National League for Democracy (NLD) as the NLD's Central Executive Committee had rejected the application of most of the 88 generation candidates on the party's electoral list. In the absence of a successor, this move by Daw Suu had shocked many well-wishers of her party at home and abroad. When questioned on this, Suu replied that the party has already decided on its Presidential candidate. He/she will be a civilian leader from NLD. In its 28-paged Manifesto, the party had pledged to amend the 2008 Constitution, hold political dialogue to address the root causes of ethnic conflicts, revamp the education system of the country and commit to an increase in the health budget. It indicated a softer line towards the military despite suffering years of torture and persecution by them. Of the 76 parties that contested the polls this year, the ethnic parties constituted two-third of them—the largest being the Shan National Democratic Party which ranks third after the NLD and the Union Solidarity for Development Party (USDP).

Third involved the ouster of one of the most potent candidate of the upcoming elections, Thura Shwe Mann, from the USDP leadership. This had confirmed President Thein Sein's desire to run for a second term in office. Shwe Mann, also the Parliament Speaker, had been replaced by the Vice-Chairman, Htay Oo after a midnight police swoop on the party headquarters. Although there have been no public explanations on Shwe Mann's ouster, speculations were ripe that tensions had been building for months between Thein Sein and Shwe Mann. The men, both retired army generals, had expressed interest in leading the country. While Thein Sein retained the support of the armed forces of the country despite lucrative reforms, Shwe Mann's relationship with the military had deteriorated steadily over the past one year. Seen as a reformist and as an ally of Aung San Suu Kyi, he was accused by the military MPs of creating "misunderstandings" between the public and the armed forces (following his support for a call in Parliament to amend Article 436 of the Constitution, which gives the military the power to veto all amendments).

Other fears revolved around the 'free-and-fairness of the 8 November elections; as one student of the Yangon University said: *We don't think they'll be constitutional. They'll be more like the elections in 1990, where Aung San Suu Kyi won, but she didn't become the leader. They weren't free and fair.*[2] The 2008 Constitution sets out a complex process whereby the *Hluttaw* (Parliament) chooses a President. Though the elections were held in November, it's likely to be March 2016 when the final sorting will take place. And the suggested electoral system (in late November 2014, a vote in the *Hluttaw*, following the advice from the Constitutional Court, endorsed a motion to stick with the current 'first-past-the-post' system over a proportional or hybrid system) does not remove the concerns as to how the USDP and the *Tatmadow* would react to a landslide electoral victory by the NLD. In the run up to the elections, other lacunae came in the form of an inadequate voter's list. Dead people had been listed and many of those alive had not been included in it. Earlier in a Press Statement, the Election Commission himself said that he was responsible for only 30 percent of the voters list. An expat in Japan who came to cast his vote in advance complained on his *Facebook* page, thus: "I came to cast three votes here, but I could not get the major vote of the Lower House. I'm from South Okkalapa in Yangon. An embassy officer said there was no Lower House ballot. We asked but we didn't get any proper answer.[3] "It's very clear," said Larry Diamond, "that democracy is not going to be achieved fully in the November elections. There are many obstacles that are going to remain over a long period of time, and it will need good strategy, a lot of persistence, courage and willingness to push democratic reforms in the face of complicated set of obstacles."[4]

Obstacles surrounding the prospect of a comprehensive peace settlement with the armed ethnic groups in the country. Though on 7 August 2015, the Union government, the *Hluttaw*, the *Tatmadow* and the Ethnic Armed Organisations finalised the text of the Nationwide Ceasefire Agreement and the excerpts of the agreement, most scholars believe that a meaningful national political dialogue is still not forthcoming. "In part," says Michael C. Williams, "this is because the Kachins and the other minorities are waiting to see what the most important election in the country's history will bring at the end of 2015."[5] But regardless of that political outcome, the capabilities of the central government in addressing the many challenges confronting it are still questionable. There's the burning Rohingya issue in the Rakhine state (and that related to Buddhist nationalism); the political system being explicitly weighted towards the military; institutional capacity being weak; dividends from economic liberalisation are not yet a top–down process; education reform, demands of artists and jade workers, women's right, transport infrastructure, electricity and connectivity have not picked up their necessitated speed. This year's flood was recognised as the country's worst natural disaster since Cyclone *Nargis* hit the country in 2008, with many people left on their own to devise the means of their survival (as the authorities failed to promptly handle the crisis).[6]

Overall, it's up to Myanmar to decide on the way it wants to work towards a 'disciplined flourishing democracy' and how much it will make it a top–down approach with a wider space for the rule of law and civil liberty. It can draw lessons from India's 'long tryst with democracy'—its electoral process; unique experience in the area of federalism; operations of an independent judiciary and media as its fourth wing of the government. Although, history shows that Myanmar has adhered to its 'Policy of Neutrality' by avoiding any influence from the outside world and that it has refrained from taking sides whenever it came to a conflict between nations. As a result of this strict neutrality, Myanmar from 1962 to 1988, became the nation with the longest history of internal armed conflict—the least developed nation with an immense debt and poverty.[7]

However, in the present context, anyone closely watching Myanmar would never want it to 'whither' away to a repressive military rule anymore. And everyone would wish that the 'transition' would take the reform process forward; that the polls would be the most credible since 1990 (amid international observers) and the country's future President would work for a meaningful dialogue and sustainable peace with the ethnic and religious communities. As Larry Diamond in his interview, pithily said: "*If this transition turns out to be fraud...people are not simply going to take this happily and say, 'Okay, you rigged your way back into power and we're just going to go about our daily business.' People are going to be angry and upset, inside Burma and outside Burma.*"[8]

Outside Myanmar, it would definitely upset a vibrant scholarly community that after the 2010 elections has found a reason to explore and study this country often tagged as "blessed with and bedeviled by diversity";[9] A community that is increasingly growing in numbers at the international conferences/workshops and is busy debating (competing) on issues as varied as democracy and FDI in Myanmar; jade trade, the *Nats* of remote villages; gender equality/diaspora and communal festivals as a means of fostering social cohesion in the country (to name a few).

In fact, anything less than a viable transition in Myanmar would seriously upset the Buddhist doctrine of *Kalama Sutta,* a teaching that many democratic activists in Myanmar have revered and which General Aung San strongly championed. In this *Sutta,* the leaders of the *Kalama* people were confronted by many different doctrines and were confused as to which were actually correct. The Buddha advised them not to accept something as truth merely because of tradition or because their parents or teachers had told them that it was true, or because it gave them immediate pleasure or even because the Buddha himself preached it. They should examine it and only when they themselves have determined that it is true, should they accept it as truth—a doctrine openly based on 'free choice'; the ideal of 'free choice' that has been long 'absent' from the Myanmarese society ruled by an oppressive military government for most of its past 50 years and one that is being misused by some Buddhists activists to suppress the minority religions in the country (like the ones induced by the 1969 movement and the MaBaTha).

For the countries in the neighbourhood and in the region, as well as the extra-regional partners, it is a 'wait and watch' situation. One important concern here relates to the fact as to how Myanmar balances its relationship with China, given that on the one hand it has suspended the Myitsone dam project (to slow down Myanmar's one-sided dependence on China for economic advantage) while on the other it has permitted the Chinese to lay down a gas pipeline at Kyaukphyu (while also allowing the Chinese to build an oil pipeline alongside the existing gas pipeline to reduce its sole reliance on the Malacca Straits). According to Chinese experts the frequent high-level visits by members of Myanmar's officialdom, including the first-ever high-level visit to China by Myanmar's opposition leader Daw Aung San Suu Kyi before the general elections highlight the fact that Beijing is willing to work with whoever is in power in Myanmar while pursuing its joint efforts to propel pragmatic cooperation and enrich the content of China-Myanmar friendship (by adhering to it non-interference principle in foreign policy). "Myanmar, in the present context," said Daw Suu "would look for good relations with both the neighbors—China and India".

India, on its behalf, will continue pursuing a *'hedging strategy'* in its foreign policy. First, New Delhi is recalibrating its strategic closeness with the United States: second, rather than balancing China through external help, New Delhi has been trying to normalise its relationship with Beijing and third, it is keen on forming a localised balance of power by increasing its defence and people-to-people contact with the middle and small powers in the region.[10] This strategy is being motivated by Prime Minister Narendra Modi's 'neighbourhood-first policy' and a proactive foreign policy based on a clear sense of priorities. According to the Foreign Secretary S. Jaishankar, there have been five "innovations" in the way India has been using its tools of statecraft to further its proactive foreign policy: narratives; lexicon and imagery; soft power; the Indian diaspora and the link between foreign policy and national development.[11] First, the Modi government has been busy developing a narrative as part of the transition in India's foreign policy. This being reflective in India's reference to its sacrifices during the First World War, or its records in the peacekeeping operations and in the humanitarian assistance and disaster relief. Second, the creation of a new lexicon and imagery through the propagation of the *Act East* policy. Third, the use of soft power in India's foreign policy as evidenced by its observance of the International Day of Yoga and in boosting religious tourism. Fourth, 'innovation' being related to engaging the overseas Indians in the development agenda of the country. And finally, using its foreign relationships to bring resources, technology and best practices to further its *Make in India* project and in furthering the national interest of the country.[12] This national interest factor is playing strongly in India's Myanmar policy as it aims to use its close relationship with that country to push its *Act East* policy by opening connectivity and business opportunities for its Northeastern states, as also to deny a safe haven to the Northeastern insurgents using the Myanmarese soil to launch attacks on India. On Indian military operations against Naga rebels inside Myanmar, Daw Suu Kyi in her television interview demanded 'complete transparency'. Suu Kyi said India must come to a settlement with the Naga rebels and Myanmar should do the same with those active on their territory and border.

For other neighboring countries like Thailand and Bangladesh, although bilateral relationship between them and Myanmar have fluctuated between conflict/ignorance and cooperation, both the neighbors are now more intent on pursuing a cooperative trade policy with Naypyidaw, since the country declared itself a 'democracy'. With regard to regional organizations like the Association of Southeast Asian Nations (ASEAN), Myanmar, as the ASEAN Chair last year has "done a good job in maintaining ASEAN centrality and unity on key issues." But, it astutely 'shelved' the complicated disputes over the South China Sea and its own human rights record by highlighting the issues of general global concern—climate change, trans-border crime, human trafficking and terrorism—which sound good to raise and do not ruffle any local feathers.[13]

Extra-regional partners like the US have extended its economic sanctions against Myanmar for another year. While President Obama's administration has heavily invested in the democratization of the country, this decision was driven by concerns over the plight of the Rohingyas. According to Priscilla Clapp: *"Myanmar's journey from deeply entrenched military oppression to sustainable democracy is long and winding and we cannot expect it to be accomplished overnight...If the US wishes to assist in tackling the country's deep-seated problems—it must remain engaged and not relegate itself to the sidelines with re-imposition of sanctions."*[14] Myanmar, despite its inward-looking nature had invited each of its neighbors in the 10-nation regional bloc to send a pair of observers to the elections and extended the offer to its dialogue partners Australia, Canada, China, the European Union, India, Japan, New Zealand, South Korea, Russia and the United States. American observers had teamed up with their ASEAN colleagues to ensure as much coverage as possible of the 8,324 polling stations involved in voting. It's only time to quietly watch and wish for real democratic transition in the country. However, post November elections and post NLD's landslide victory, the country still has to keep certain serious 'issues' in mind before the final selection of its new President in March 2016.

One among them is the way in which it will tackle the vested interests of powerful sections of the military in the administration: remove the institutional barriers originating from controversial articles in the Constitution: the way the country will take its economic progress forward through the involvement of people from all sections of the society: how will it handle its ethnic issues, grievances of minorities and growing influence of Buddhist nationalist forces underneath: and how will NLD share power as the Constitution bars Daw Suu from becoming the President of the country (yet she vowed to make all decisions as leader of the party).

Nay Zin Latt, a former army officer and government adviser, rightly pointed out: "...the military shared a vision of the army's withdrawing from politics, but the question is how fast. Their mission is to become a professional army". "But it's not easy. Habits are deeply rooted." "We need stability. In America, you have spent over 200 years to get to where you are. This is the very beginning stage of our transition."[16]

## NOTES

1. Daw Aung San Suu Kyi's interview with Karan Thapar on India Today Television show *To the Point*, 2015.
2. Timothy Simson, "Have Myanmar's Generals turned Aung San Suu Kyi into a Lame Duck in Wolf's Clothing?" asiapacific.anu.edu.au/2015/08/12 [A.0. 24-8-2015]
3. Min Zin, "Is Burma's Opposition Ready for the Post-Suu Kyi Era?" www.irrawaddy.org [A.0. 24-8-2015]
4. Nicholas Farelly quoting Larry Diamond's interview at the University of Yangon's Department of International Relations, "Will Myanmar's People be Key to a Successful Transition?" asiapacific.anu.edu.au {A.O. 21-8-2015]
5. http://www.elevenmyanmar.com/politics/vote-fraud-or-vote-theft-rigging-responsible-person-u-tin-aye-should-give-clear [A.O, 3 September 2015]
6. Larry Diamond, "Democracy is not Going To be Achieved Fully in the November Elections", http://www.irrawaddy.org/interview/larry-diamond-democracy-is-not-going-to-be-achieved-fully-in-the-november elections.html [A.O. 21-8-2015]
7. Michael C. Williams, "Myanmar's Troubled Path to Reform: Political Prospects in a Landmark Election Year", Research Presented at Chatham House, Asia Programme, February 2015.
8. Ibid. Also see Nicholas Farrelly, "Politics of Disaster", asiapacific.anu.edu.au {A.O. 18-8-2015]
9. Larry Diamond, "Democracy is not Going To be Achieved Fully in the November Elections", http://www.irrawaddy.org/interview/larry-diamond-democracy-is-not-going-to-be-achieved-fully-in-the-november elections.html {A.O. 21-8-2015]
10. Martin Smith, *Burma: Insurgency and the Politics of Ethnicity* (London: Zed Books, 1991).
11. Harsh V.Pant and Yogesh Joshi, "Indian Foreign Policy Responds to the US Pivot", *Asia Policy*, No. 19 (January 2015), 89-114.
12. Prashnath Parameswaran, "A New 'Proactive' Indian Foreign Policy under Modi", thediplomat.com/2015/07 [A.O. 20-8-2015]
13. Ibid.
14. Nyan Lynn Aung, "Myanmar Quietly gets the Job Done", *The Myanmar Times*, January 2015.

15. Priscilla Clapp, "Myanmar: Taking the Long View", *Asia Pacific Bulletin*, No. 286, November 2014.
16. http://www.nytimes.com/2015/12/03/world/asia/myanmar-aung-san-suu-kyi-meets-president-army.html?_r=Also see http://www.lse.ac.uk/newsAndMedia/videoAndAudio/channels/publicLecturesAndEvents/player.aspx?id=3217

# Index